The Politics of Freedom

Jeroen Zandberg

2011

ISBN   978-1-4477-9378-6

NUR   754

Table of Contents

1. INTRODUCTION

This book is about freedom. What it is and how to get it. Freedom of expression, freedom of association, freedom to strive for all positions in society without a self appointed elite being able to close off opportunities and above all the freedom to live the best possible life of your choosing. In order to achieve this freedom society has to be organised in such a way that the institutions and laws promote freedom. The chapters in this book provide an answer to how modern democratic society should be organised to promote freedom. The values of the Enlightenment are hereby carefully examined and interpreted to help us in our quest. It provides the tools to take charge of our own destiny.

The second chapter investigates the **principle of equality** to note that in our society it is unfortunately not a principle at all because many laws and left-wing interpretations of these laws actively discriminate. The policy of diversity and multiculturalism is the modern equivalent of Apartheid whereby people are labelled and provided positions within society on the basis of a certain characteristic like race or gender. Laws based on this left-wing ideology have created a society which is less diverse then it would have been if everyone was treated as an individual. Diversity doesn't require foreigners, only individuals.

The next chapter describes **self-determination**. Without self-determination every individual is the slave of a higher power. Left-wing policy actively tries to minimize self-determination of people in favour of a large government, controlled by a left-wing elite. An essential element of the left-wing world view is the idea of one moral truth. Through rational thought all reasonable people will come to the same (left-wing) conclusion. Everyone with a different opinion is either stupid and unreasonable or an evil person. A second element in undermining self-determination of the people is the idea of the emancipation of the common man by the elite. The common man is thereby incapable of deciding his own fate and desires, which should therefore be in the hands of a small left-wing elite. These false reasons lay at the core of left-wing ideology.

The fourth chapter investigates **tolerance**. Tolerance revolves around allowing different opinions and lifestyles to co-exist. The bigger the possible differences within a community the more tolerant society can/has to be. A culture consisting of a large number of individuals has more possible differences than a multicultural environment with only a few competing groups. Therefore there is more tolerance in the former than the latter. The only thing that tolerance can't tolerate is a threat to the continued existence of the community.

The **Rule of Law** is the subject of the fifth chapter. Rules are never just rules but always interpretations and therefore always political. The left-wing elite might no longer control the majority in much of politics but still has a firm grip on the legal systems. Due to the fact that judges are not democratically checked and that their personal opinions are often crucial in their verdicts make for an enormous democratic deficit. It is crucial that the judiciary is placed under the control of the people. Hereby we need to see the separation of powers as a means to prevent one elite to monopolize all power. It is not directed at preventing the people to gain control.

The sixth chapter discusses the **freedom of expression**. Freedom of expression includes every opinion that can help society in their quest for truth. A debate eventually leads to a truth that is consequently transformed into policy by the government. When it becomes impossible to participate in the public debate democracy ceases to exist. The gravest threat to a democratic society is violence and the threat of violence that closes off the public domain for the population whereby it is no longer possible to have an open debate.

The seventh chapter focuses on **democracy**. Democracy is a procedure to come to a Truth, whereby the democracy in itself has no objective other than the creation of the public domain in order to make the search for Truth possible. This public domain has to create an environment in which all persons have the ability to participate in the public debate as equals in order to get to the best possible truth together. To this end the public domain should not be based on a morality and should also be devoid of power. The conclusion that follows from this theory is that democratic procedures should be a-moral and without objective. When people decide to justify and legitimate the democratic procedures by formulating an objective for them, then democracy itself is denied and should therefore be seen as an undemocratic act. It is then not the people that rule but it is a certain Truth that rules. A democracy can therefore not be based on a Truth but should instead be undetermined and empty of values. In a democratic society people will be continuously searching for new truths that are constantly being formed in the public domain ensuring that there will never be one Truth that comes to sit at the basis of democracy. In this line of thought it is assumed that any truth can be lost but that being directed at getting to the truth will always remain. This is therefore a Truth of democracy. It subsequently provides the ultimate negation of left-wing claims that their ideology should be the basis of modern Western society. If left-wing ideology governs then democracy is denied.

The **populist** quest for truth is to reason from the perspective of the people and have their best interests in mind and to create policy based on this. An important part of this populist quest for truth is to uncover hidden problems that hinder the people in making informed judgments about the situation. In such a scenario the populist politician speaks the language of the people and at the same time adds to its vocabulary, unlike the elite which speaks a different language. The populist politician can therefore be seen as a champion for the emancipation of the unrepresented whereby the 'silent majority' are given arguments to overcome the intimidation by the elite.

Populist politics understands that the existing procedures that ought to guarantee democratic debate and transfer of power have been hijacked by an elite, causing democracy to disappear. The search for the best truth for the people can therefore only take place outside these hijacked institutions. **Populism** is about regaining democracy by circumnavigating the hijacked, and consequently dictatorial, institutions and replacing this with a direct connection with the people.

2. EQUALITY

One of the foundations of Western society is the idea of equality for all citizens. This equality is essential for democracy to be able to function properly. If people were to be unequal then debates and elections would only be theatre and the direction in which society develops will be completely determined by those who hold power, at the expense of the less powerful.

In analyzing equality we need to take the interests of each individual into account. When someone has the aptitude to become a professional wrestler then it would be unethical to force him to take ballet lessons. Else his chances of a successful life (his evolutionary fitness) would be sacrificed for an ideal that has been formulated by an elite in order for them to hold on to power.

Equality does not mean that everyone has or should have the same genetic make-up and social position. Equality revolves around the equal value of each individual whereby this value is determined from the perspective of the individual itself. The key to equality is therefore to offer equal chances to each individual to strive for his personal success.

2.1 Equality as principle

An important principle of Western culture is the democratic constitutional state and the principle of equality whereby every person is seen as an individual with equal rights. This is clearly reflected in article one of the Dutch constitution.

> **"All people on the territory of the Netherlands will be judged equally in equal circumstances. Discrimination**

on the basis of religion, philosophy of life, political views, race, gender or any other basis is not allowed."[i]

It appears as if equality as a principle is strongly established in Dutch law. Unfortunately, this is not the case. Other laws make exceptions to the implementation of equality as a principle. There is for example the law called General Law for Equal Treatment which makes it possible to distinguish between groups.

> "The prohibition of discrimination as laid out in this law does not apply when the discrimination concerns a specific measure that has as its objective to privilege women or persons from a specific ethnic or cultural minority in order to correct disadvantages caused by race or gender and that these discriminatory measures are in a reasonable relation to the ultimate objective."[ii]

The mere fact that the General Law for Equal Treatment makes exceptions on when the principle of equality is implemented means that equality is not a genuine principle in Dutch law. A principle can't be founded on another principle else it would not be a principle at all. One of the most fundamental values of the Enlightenment is therefore denied and replaced by another principle.

> "My problem with the *leader of the right-wing populist party*, and this is so crucial that I don't want to cooperate with him, is that he makes distinctions between people based on race and culture. He undermines the foundations of our democratic constitutional state."[iii]

An important left-wing claim against right-wing populists is that the democratic constitutional state is under siege because the latter wants to make distinctions based on religion, ethnicity or other group characteristics. This should be enough reason to exclude right-wing populists from the public debate. Interestingly enough it is the left-wing that makes distinctions based on ethnicity and other group characteristics and has even made it law. It is therefore the left-wing that undermines the foundations of our democratic constitutional state and the principle of equality.

How do you determine what the impact of race or gender is on the current distribution of positions in society? The assumed disadvantages that people encounter because of their race or gender are mainly based on left-wing prejudice. The left-wing also assumes that all white men have a good position in society and that they received these because they are white and male. It is highly questionable if that assumption is correct. The 'principle' of equality is then interpreted by the left-wing to fit their best interests. Interpretation means that there is only one principle at work and that is the principle of power. It is therefore the principle of power (of the elite) that is taken as principle and foundation of the 'democratic constitutional state'.

2.2 The intrinsic value of people

The General Law for Equal Treatment is actively promoted by the government, civil society and businesses. The policy of diversity and positive discrimination are important spearheads in the distribution of high social positions. The starting point herewith is that in the minds of the left-wing elite a diverse environment has added value. This indicates that a diverse environment has greater value than a homogenous one. Diversity is hereby seen as a mix of men and women who have various cultural backgrounds. A homogenous environment is seen as an environment dominated by white men. The plans to come to greater diversity assume that the current situation is a homogenous white men's culture.

Western culture holds the equality of people to be an important characteristic of society, whereby all people have equal worth. This doesn't mean that society is devoid of hierarchy. A hierarchy implies a difference in value. These differences are tolerated and legitimated by the fact that they are the result of acquired characteristics like education, ambition and work ethics, instead of innate characteristics.

The General Law for Equal Treatment and all related left-wing ideologies deny this equality and assume that innate characteristics like gender and ethnicity are in itself values. According to left-wing ideology, whether a person has blue or brown eyes determines to a great extent the value of that person.

> **"In meetings women are generally more efficient and less focussed on power play and their ego. I am convinced that a meeting is shorter with many women present. It is shorter and more effective."**[iv]

Another argument to promote positive discrimination is that it is an added value to be a woman. A woman has qualities that a man lacks. Furthermore, the mere presence of women improves the entire social environment. This is another added value of women. This line of reasoning is based on prejudices about men and women. It is highly questionable whether it correctly describes reality. It also denies the existence of the individual and only assumes the presence of a few groups: men, women and foreigners, which is a degradation of true diversity. Instead of millions of different individuals, left-wing ideologues know only a few group differences.

The labelling of people on the basis of their perceived intrinsic value is comparable to the ideology of colonialism. It is therefore the opposite of the Enlightenment that awards each person with the same intrinsic value and which stands at the basis of our vision of a just society and human rights. Left-wing ideology is driven by hatred against everything that is Western, white and male.

> **"The diversity in society is not the planned outcome of specific policy. It is a natural consequence of modern society in which we travel far and live elsewhere; and not just us. That diversity is like wine and provides taste to our society. If I would only encounter clones of myself [white men] when walking in the street then it would not be worthwhile to go outside."[v]**

The above remark by the Dutch minister of Internal Affairs is a good example of left-wing reasoning which is a result of alienation from society and dehumanisation of the other. It claims that an environment consisting of white men/people can't have diversity and that foreigners are needed to achieve this. However, in a liberal society diversity requires only individuals. Left-wing ideology considers all Europeans to be interchangeable like a 19th century colonial who only saw *Negro's* in Africa. Not the individual with his or her personality, dreams and desires but only an imagined stereotype is seen. This shows the left-wing mix of racism and contempt for individualism. In individualism all people are considered unique regardless of their innate characteristics. Equality is hereby essential else there can be no individualism. When people are deemed intrinsically unequal then it is the relations of power between them that is the deciding factor in determining what choices people have and what position they will hold in society.

The idea of intrinsic equality of people is best explained by Immanuel Kant who stated that people are not a means to an end but an end in themselves. This idea stands at the basis of Western ideas of a fair society. When we instead don't take individual persons as ends in themselves but as a means to achieve another objective, namely diversity, then we deny an essential part of what a fair society is. According to Western ethics it is immoral to sacrifice others in order to achieve an ideal society. The important 19th and 20th century ideological competitors of Western democracy, like communism, National Socialism and fascism were to a great extent based on the principle of sacrificing others for an ideal and the idea that man is only a means to a greater end. The presence of a policy of diversity and positive discrimination corrupts society to such an extent that it sacrifices the essence of the democratic constitutional state and with it denies equality, individualism and human rights.

2.3 People oriented versus task oriented

Many arguments in favour of diversity also claim that it improves the competitiveness of both individual businesses as well as society at large. According to left-wing science diversity creates a stronger and more creative society. A homogeneous group is then less able to make proper decisions because their views are narrow and limited. A heterogeneous group would then have a broader view and be more open to alternatives. This opinion is also supported by much scientific evidence, which unfortunately was not done by proper scientists but instead by political activists.

However, it is not the similarity of people within a group that is the cause of a limited perspective, it is the focus on the group and person itself instead of the focus on the market and the tasks at hand, which causes the narrowing of peoples' views. Being self-centred is always a bad recipe for success. The banking crisis was for example not caused by a monoculture of white fifty-year old men, but by a culture of self-enrichment whereby people were detached from society. A policy of diversity will not be able to prevent this. On the contrary, because a company which is directed at the intrinsic value of its employees, instead of the proper execution of corporate tasks, will descent into political chaos and eventually disintegrates. Ironically, the focus on interpersonal relations leads to political power play.

The illusion of diversity as an added value also comes to the fore in the iron works company which was the winner of the 2008 Dutch diversity price. Let's hope this prize does not reflect in the finished product. When you can distinguish an iron works product made by an immigrant from Somalia from that made by an Iraqi then you have diversity but also bad management. There are only two kinds of finished products; a good or a bad one. Diversity is also a poor strategy for success.

Another rebuttal of diversity as an added value and something to strive for is that when a group of young people of different backgrounds follow a traineeship at a major company they all end up looking virtually identical. An important aspect in this is that the proper execution of a certain task can only be done in a limited number of ways. Furthermore, being different from others is not simply positive. It implies a hierarchy which leads to conflict within the group. Power play within a group can be very destructive for this group. From the perspective of the individual, being different is good when you are better at something. If not, you are excluded and oppressed.

When we take a critical look at the 'scientific' evidence on diversity and homogeneity it appears that homogeneity does lead to much creativity. Some of the most creative countries, like Japan and Finland, are still very homogenous and are focussed on the international market. A preliminary conclusion is therefore that the most creative groups are homogenous and focussed on a diverse outside environment.

> **"It is a simple business case. In order to provide the best service to our customers we also have to be a reflection of them."[vi]**

> **"Diversity means that we as an organisation need to be a cross-section of society."[vii]**

Another (deliberate) error in judgment is that an organisation needs to be a cross-section of its customers and society. Every multi-national proves this argument wrong. SONY for example is a global company from Japan with many departments in as many different countries. However, because it is global doesn't mean that the workforce is a cross-section of the world's population. This is also not necessary because any respectable company doesn't rely on the local gossip in the downtown bar, but does professional market research in order to plan its business strategy. The idea that a company should be a reflection of its customers is therefore an example of provincialism. Secondly, it denies the principle of individualism. In a society of sixteen million individuals you can only be a cross-section of society if the company has sixteen million employees. Furthermore, it is also an indication that the mutual trust in society has disappeared. People don't see the other person as equal anymore and trust has broken down. The zero-sum competition makes people to suspect that everyone is out to get him, which in fact is true. A policy of diversity makes these problems even greater. Eventually this can lead to a situation similar to that in many developing countries, whereby people only recognise the authority of their own clan and dehumanize everyone else. A way towards a solution to this problem is to focus on the tasks and not on people because the latter implies oppression.

2.4 Integration as a process and not an endpoint

The objective of diversity and affirmative action policies is often taken to be 'integration'. With the term 'integration' is then meant that non-natives become fully part of society and can therefore no longer be distinguished as a separate group. They are then 'integrated'. In order to achieve this objective a policy of active support to accommodate newcomers to gain a good position in society needs to be implemented.

The left-wing argument is as follows. Immigrants usually start from a disadvantage due to a different culture, lower education and a limited network. This disadvantage then needs to be removed by providing them special benefits not given to the native population. If that were not to happen then there is a chance of a social Apartheid system between Europeans and foreigners. A policy of affirmative action is then one of the trademarks of integration.

A major ethical problem with the previous argument is that it goes against the principle of equality which is so crucial to Western society. Individuals from outside of Europe are then privileged compared to native individuals. The former are therefore given a higher intrinsic value compared to the latter. Western society is not based on groups but on individuals who each individually compete for their position in society. A foreign individual is then privileged for the mere fact that he/she is foreign. This has major consequences for Western society. There is always integration and disintegration in an individualistic society regardless of the presence of foreigners. Each individual strives to obtain the best possible social position and self-development, which can sometimes come at the expense of others. In Western society this is always accompanied by conflict between individuals who consequently drift apart and cause society to disintegrate. In order to keep the community intact there need to be mechanisms to keep these individuals together. The nation-state, representing and imposing a distinct national culture, has historically proven to be the best suited mechanism for this purpose. Integration and disintegration are eternal processes and there will therefore still be integration in the year 2525 even if all of humanity would have miraculously been transformed into one single community.

The fact that integration is an everlasting process and not a fixed endpoint has major consequences for individuals in Europe. By privileging foreigners you automatically discriminate Europeans. Due to the fact that competition in Western society is individualistic means that all Europeans who are not fortunate enough to belong to the elite happy few will be limited in their opportunities and simply have to accept being second class citizens. The opportunities of Europeans are then sacrificed to give those opportunities to foreigners. It is hereby also not possible to make the cake bigger so each can take his fare share. Every modern society has a hierarchy in which the top offers better opportunities for survival then the bottom. Forming a family and raising children requires a stable and good social position. The chaos and desperation of broken families on welfare gives a good insight into what happens when people are on the lowest steps of the social ladder. It means that it is important to get a good position in society if you wish to survive. Due to unfair competition as a result of integration policies, the survival of ordinary Europeans is at stake. Another policy which aggravates this situation even further is that the same people who advocate integration and affirmative action also try to keep the borders open. Seeing that every newcomer needs to be assisted to integrate into society, the resulting system will be Apartheid which privileges foreigners. The eventual consequence will be a replacement of the native European population. Integration can therefore best be compared to a neutron bomb which leaves the structures intact but destroys all people living within it.

If we don't want to sacrifice the European people to a deliberately incorrectly interpreted abstract ideal then integration has to occur on an individualistic basis. No distinction should therefore be made between Europeans and foreigners. On average it is the case that Europeans have the home advantage because they make up and are therefore part of European culture, but this can't be a valid argument to privilege foreigners. Immigrants migrated to Europe because they thought they would have better opportunities compared to their native lands. It is a completely reasonable requirement that if you move to another country you go and live according to the rules of that new home. Through hard work and by accepting the new culture as their own, immigrants will eventually gain all the benefits of being part of European culture. Holding on to ones' own culture is then mostly a will to power in order to gain a top position without the need to work hard for it.

Immigrants freely choose to move to Europe. If they don't feel at home then the best and quickest solution is to move to a country that has the desired cultural identity. According to left-wing liberal logic this should not be a problem because migration is in their reasoning a force of nature. A fundamentalist Muslim who wants to impose Sharia law in Europe is therefore completely free, after he receives his monthly welfare check, to take a plane to Saudi Arabia and live in the desert according to the principles of Islam.

If we accept the fact that culture plays an important role in the success of a society then it is highly questionable that we should replace European culture with those of countries in which technological development has been stagnant for centuries. Furthermore, it is not necessary to import immigrants for European culture to adapt to modern challenges. According to left-wing liberal logic it would be impossible to eat potatoes, because they originally come from Peru. Only if there is a large immigration of Peruvians can Europeans eat potatoes. False reasoning like this is present everywhere and is used to undermine European culture. It is the result of self-hatred and alienation of the left-wing elite. It goes without question that we can learn from other nations and cultures, but it doesn't mean that European culture should be destroyed.

The right-wing political spectrum is often associated with the idea that there are clearly defined peoples and ideals like racial purity. The left-wing liberal worldview has similar arguments about a perceived purity that disappears due to current migration. According to left-wing liberal fatalistic views the European population will inevitable be destroyed because there will always be migration. It is however not a threat to the survival of the European population if there is immigration of individuals. The major threat comes from mass-immigration combined with 'integration', which can result in a replacement of the European population with newcomers. It is not the conservation of an imagined purity, but survival that is at stake. People who react against foreigners are not worried whether their son or daughter comes home with a foreigner as partner. They are worried that their son or daughter doesn't come home at all or isn't able to form a family. Racism only comes to the fore when people sense that their survival is at stake when a competing ethnic group makes their lives impossible.

2.5 Distributive justice

> "What holds women back when they join an organisation is that there are already established structures as well as an *old boys network*."[viii]

> "Women who have finished their higher education are often convinced that they can conquer the world. If they enter an organisation whereby everything is not as easy and straightforward as previously assumed they quickly lose self-confidence."[ix]

With these remarks and the context in which they are done the articles argue that women are confronted with structures within organisations that make it hard for them to immediately reach the top. This consequently is unfair. This line of left-wing reasoning is a clear case of selective blindness because this situation is encountered by everyone. A competitive structure which is different from student life. An established network of people who hold the positions of power and have more knowledge and experience. These are normal characteristics of every working environment and should not be casually thrown out the window to replace it with the atmosphere of a bar or club. The ability of people to move up in an organisation as well as enhancing self-confidence are good elements but they should not be focussed solely on a small group of highly educated women from the aristocracy. It would de-legitimate the structures itself and disadvantage a large part of the population. Despite the left-wing prejudices not every white man is a multimillionaire and part of the old boys network. This left-wing worldview is mostly due to how they organise the world; the left-wing *old boys and girls network.*

2.5.1 Unfair redistribution

Those who plead for more diversity act from the idea that this would make society more just. Of course this is a left-wing interpretation of a just society which is clearly visible in the ideal (but which is by definition never implemented) of emancipating the lower classes as well as the rejection and contempt of European culture. In this way they acknowledge that the policy of increasing diversity is discriminatory but that it is necessary and morally just in order to compensate for historical wrongs. In the past, women and foreigners were discriminated and in order to undo this wrong it is necessary to positively discriminate them. Such a left-wing interpretation can never be quantified because how much discrimination has history seen and what are the consequences of it today? In light of the fact that history is always an interpretation and says more about the present then the past means that this kind of historical injustice is merely a left-wing construction to legitimate a desired social structure. They also make the (deliberate) false reasoning that society consists of only a few groups and not millions of individuals. The policy of diversity is the last convulsion of the multicultural ideal of distinct ethnic groups that co-exist side by side in a system governed by a left-wing elite.

Besides denying the individuality of people they are also dehumanized. Are all Europeans and all men multimillionaires? When we look at the way in which diversity policy is implemented we clearly see that the ideal of emancipating the less fortunate only includes a small group, deliberately chosen by the elite. This small group includes well-educated women and foreigners with a specific lifestyle and political worldview. It is remarkable how uniform an environment becomes when it falls victim to diversity policy. The more policies to implement diversity the less actual diversity there is. Diversity often comes down to a marketing trick to have only young, hip and likeminded people and exclude everyone else. Those people, be they men, women or foreigner, from a socially less well off position are on the other hand not supported. Diversity policy is therefore strongly elitist.

The simplistic argument that the left-wing elite uses to legitimize diversity policy goes like this: half of the population consists of women and all (important) positions in society therefore need to be filled equally by women. At this moment not all jobs are equally distributed between men and women. Especially the number of women in top positions is found important. This is then a legitimate reason to have a policy of active discrimination. The cause of women being underrepresented is according to left-wing theory the result of deliberate exclusion and a lack of knowledge and opportunities of women. Left-wing ideology states that all men and women are identical. Consequently there is a need for specific laws that provide women with top positions instead of men. In order to come to a left-wing fair society men should be excluded because else they would exclude women.

The problem with left-wing reasoning is that it has never been proven and is only a collection of left-wing prejudices. For example, we could use the same scenario for groups that are more successful then the average European. According to left-wing logic the Jews should be actively excluded from top positions because they have a better social position then the average European. All people are identical and because there are more Jews in high positions they therefore deliberately exclude others, etcetera.

The 'current situation', 'history' and 'diversity policy' are all false arguments that are used to implement policy in support of left-wing ideals. In order to see how we should implement a fair social system we should re-examine the Enlightenment and the principle of the individual as basis of policy. When we try to judge people by their personal abilities then we come a lot closer to a fair distribution. When a person has the talent to become a wrestler you should not force him to take ballet lessons because you would degrade his potential for success. It is up to every individual to get the maximum out of his or her life, whereby the state should guarantee that there are no rules that exclude people. Diversity policy on the other hand consists of regulations meant to exclude people from their personal success. For that reason alone it should be outlawed.

2.5.2 A policy of diversity results in corruption

A consequence of the policy of diversity is that the structures that enable individuals to strive towards a successful career are degraded. We build upon the accomplishments of our ancestors. The institutional framework that we constructed through the centuries enables us to increase our abilities to survive. If these structures no longer improve our chances of success then they work against us and as such cause great harm in our pursuit for success.

In an environment determined by the policy of diversity the ability to get a proper job is no longer dependent on objective, measurable qualities. The left-wing argument is, correctly, that top positions are often granted to people because of their relations with those in power who distribute wealth among themselves. The core business of the top (or elite) is thereby unfortunately not the presence of specific knowledge about a certain field but to gain and hold on to power. The battle for top positions is therefore always political. Unfortunately, the left-wing ideologues abuse this unfair situation. They don't try to make the system more just, but instead increase the injustice of the system by adding another unfair variable into the equation. The left-wing ideology is not to judge people on their skills at all but to select them on other, not directly relevant for the job, characteristics.

When you are no longer rewarded on the basis of your performance but only on an intrinsic value and other non-quantifiable characteristics then it is foolish to work hard because the profit from your hard work goes to others. The only viable option to this exclusion is to create an informal network yourself whereby you can't focus on executing the specific job but instead must focus on personal relations of power. This creates a left-wing society whereby people are placed against each other and all progress stops. The motivation to create new and unique things that might eventually offer a personal reward disappears completely.

The policy of diversity can sometimes be successful in breaking the *old boys network*. Unfortunately, it results in a new and even stronger shady network of new *old boys and girls*. In this redistribution many will be excluded just because they don't belong to the proper 'aristocratic' families, which causes great tensions within society. It is then possible that parallel structures arise in order for those excluded to get a proper position in society. This would be a great step towards the left-wing ideal of competing elites who are far elevated above the common man. The ideal of a meritocracy, which is a society whereby people are rewarded based on merit, is then squandered in favour of a corrupted left-wing elitist alternative. A left-wing meritocracy is an aristocracy.

2.5.3 A policy of diversity increases hierarchy and inequality

In a left-wing society individual qualities are not determined by the presence of objective skills but whether or not you are a member of an exclusive club. When we select people on the basis of perceived intrinsic values instead of quantifiable and thus measurable criteria we limit the ability of talent to rise through the ranks and instead create a 'society' composed of many isolated groups. Such an environment is ideal for elites but disastrous for the rest of society. Unfortunately, Europe is becoming ever more hierarchical en thereby less democratic.

Not just the left-wing ideologues favour diversity. Part of the business elite shares similar views regarding diversity. Left-wing hobbies are then often shared by right-wing people as well. The reason for this is because the policy of diversity is an ideal tool to gain and hold on to power. The person in power is the one who determines which position is given to what person without any objective criteria to base this decision on. With the policy of diversity, power is taken from the institutional structures and placed in the hands of individuals at the top. It is thereby an ideal way to exclude potential competitors. In light of the fact that the struggle for top positions revolves around gaining and holding on to power, means that only those who don't pose a threat to the ruling elite will have the opportunity to have a successful career. For example, politicians like Italian president Berlusconi and EU chairman Barosso claim to be great advocates of diversity. They therefore select people from very diverse background in their respective cabinets. In reality they are kings who merely appoint a household of dependents.

Another, related, reason why the policy of diversity is also popular with right-wing people at the top of major companies is that it makes it easy to hide one's own incompetence. It is often the case that an executive who has been at the top for years and used to be motivated and capable in the past lost both his belief and expertise to lead the company to new heights. Competent in the past, but incompetent in the present and future. The lack of present skills forces the top executive to find other ways of legitimizing his top position. The policy of diversity is ideal for this purpose. It provides the top executive a feigned moral superiority. Through the social democratic ideology of emancipating the less well off, this legitimizes his top position, because it requires someone with high moral character to emancipate other people and provide them with opportunities.

The fact that so many top executives blindly follow the left-wing ideology of diversity shows that they are not real leaders but mere followers who bend each way the wind blows. They simply adopt ideas of others without any critical thought themselves. This is unfortunately a sign that many top executives are not fit for their job. Eventually the competitive advantage of such companies degrades and they don't survive.

A way to make sure the system of positive discrimination becomes unattractive to the elite is to change the conditions upon which this discrimination is implemented. When left-wing ideologues look at a person's background to determine his or her 'intrinsic value' they should also look at his/her social position, as well as that of his/her parents, grand-parents etcetera. It is possible to reserve top positions for women, but it is also possible to reserve top positions for women from a poor background. Something similar applies to men and ethnic minorities. This line of reasoning will remove an important element of abuse out of the system of positive discrimination. If implemented in such a way it will be unlikely that the policy of diversity will continue to receive wide support among the elite. Furthermore, it is unethical to sacrifice others for your ideals. A white man, who claims that there is a need for more diversity, meaning less white men, only has one ethical option and that is to resign from his position in favour of someone from the minority group. A better world starts with your own actions.

2.5.4 Ambitions

Personal ambition should not be limited to a specific position in a bureaucratic institution. Ambition should be seen much wider, namely the ambition to become as successful as possible in life. A job is only one part of life. Raising children or discovering the secrets of the universe are much more valuable than a managing position at a detergent company. In the end successful survival is the primary ambition.

Modern society doesn't have a rigid, absolute distinction between professions for men and women. The legal profession for example used to be primarily male, while at present the majority is already female. Such a development is not good or bad as such and also doesn't say much about the profession itself. It might be that in the past it was more profitable for men to work in legal jobs, while they now perhaps prefer other professions. The main focus should be that everyone has the ability to best guarantee his survival by pursuing the position that does him justice. Society continues to change and the relative positions change with it. It is therefore also impossible to precisely determine the policy of diversity because it could be the result of deliberate policy or due to other social- and technological developments.

An important argument against the policy of diversity is therefore that it creates a rigid society in which an elite *a priori* decides which positions should be held by whom, regardless whether this is beneficial to individual people or society. This endangers the flexibility of society and resembles that of the Soviet Union. In the Soviet Union a small elite based in the

Kremlin created five-year plans that encompassed all of society. A major problem is that this only 'works' if the objectives are known in advance. It implies that it can only be a strategy to catch up to a more advanced competitor. The main question is therefore whether we want to be followers by choosing a bureaucratic diversity oriented environment or that we try to become leaders of our own lives and shape the future ourselves.

As society we should have the ambition to approach people as an individual with equal chances to enable them to maximize their opportunities to have a good life and survive. Sacrificing others in order to achieve an imagined perfect society is always immoral. As long as the left-wing elite doesn't sacrifice its own children every policy that is based on this principle will merely be a will to power.

3. SELF-DETERMINATION

An extensive government that determines peoples' lives to a great degree makes people dependent upon the government which provides it with more power. Furthermore, it destroys the mutual bonds between people because these bonds are no longer necessary to survive. This in turn increases the power of government even further because each citizen is isolated from others and thereby becomes completely dependent on government. This left-wing ideal enables a small elite to rule over a dependent population.

The right-wing alternative on the other hand proposes a small and forceful government in order to provide people maximum freedom of movement to determine what life suits them best. The possibility for abuse of power is thereby limited while self-determination of the population is maximized.

3.1 Paternalism versus individual freedom

An essential element of the left-wing world view is the idea of one moral truth that can be attained by any rational well thinking person. Every person will come to this same (left-wing) conclusion. Everyone who has a different opinion is then either stupid, unreasonable or an evil person. The left-wing view only knows 'facts' and they speak for themselves. This left-wing rationality can in reality be better described as a rationalisation because an absolute moral truth is impossible to achieve, seeing that nature itself knows no morality. All ethics are ultimately based on unproven assumptions which are only considered true because it suits our best interests. The left-wing world view can therefore be considered a religion. Anyone with a different world view is then blaspheme and is terrorised in order to maintain the hegemony of the assumed superiority of the left-wing elite. The fact that the left-wing ideology is inevitably correct also means that other opinions are excluded from the debate because the assumptions of left-wing ideology determine the boundaries of this public debate. Anyone with a different vision is then excluded with the rationalisation that they are evil or stupid. This false reasoning by the left-wing elite is consequently responsible for the fact that a large part of the population feels that they are no longer represented. They are excluded because they are considered unfit due to the fact that they don't follow left-wing logic. In order to regain self-determination it is important to see that a moral truth can never be absolute and that the so-called 'facts' of the left-wing elite are mere opinions of the establishment that desperately clings to power.

3.1.1 Social-democracy and the redefinition of the Other

The left-wing elite claims solidarity with the less well off. Unfortunately there is often a contradiction between actions and words. For example, they promote the multi-cultural society but preferably send their children to an all white school. Furthermore, they promote homosexuality in others, but also look the other way when Muslims threaten gay rights. Finally, only a small part of those in need are truly supported. They help foreigners who do their bidding, but spit upon those excluded who happen to be European. The left-wing elite is like an American evangelical television host who lives a life of luxury thanks to the gifts of his congregation and privately indulges in all that God forbids. In the case of the left-wing elite this 'God' consists of all the principles they promote and to which everyone has to abide, except of course themselves.

A crucial element in their world view is the idea that a left-wing truth has only been revealed to a small elite while the rest remains in a dark cave. In order to save those trapped blind in their cave it is necessary to implement left-wing policy whereby all arguments and ideals only apply to the common people and not to the left-wing elite. The common man is in the eyes of the left-wing elite not capable of determining what is right or wrong. Intelligent thought is the domain of the left-wing elite. This implies an almost absolute power because the elite determines what the common man needs and wants, because they are not capable to do this themselves. This left-wing rationalisation provides almost unlimited power. These rationalisations are legitimated through the elite claim that they represent the interests of those in need, which is labelled 'good', while it is the elite that determines what the interests of those in need are and also determines what is morally good.

From the previous paragraphs it can be concluded that the left-wing elite is dependent upon the acceptance of the left-wing world view as objectively fair. When it is only seen as merely an opinion (what it by definition is) than the whole system collapses because the left-wing logic no longer applies. Furthermore, for the left-wing ideology to work it is necessary to have a group of people who are not yet enlightened and who can be guided out of their dark cave. In the past this group consisted of white factory workers while from the 1960's onward the elite decided to choose another group to emancipate. The factory workers were already emancipated which meant that a crucial element of the left-wing ideology of power fell away. On the other hand there was a sheer unlimited number of people who could be emancipated; foreigners and the entire non-Western world.

The left-wing elite has therefore redefined both those in need of assistance as well as the Other. The Other is now the white person who is so unlucky as not to be part of a small elite. It is clear from the reactions of the left-wing where their interests lie when perceived wrongs against a group of foreigners are shown.

The same wrongs are completely ignored when the victims are European. This identification with foreigners and the dehumanization of the ordinary white person is an important characteristic of the left-wing elite. The best friends of the left-wing elite, the white workers, have been replaced with foreigners. With friends like these who needs enemies. It also raises the question how reliable someone is if he sacrifices his 'friends' in order to get a better social position. Eventually the left-wing will again redefine the other when foreigners decide that they no longer want to be emancipated by the left-wing elite and instead demand freedom. This is a continuous process and comparable to capitalism which needs continuous growth to avoid collapse. An environment that combines right-wing capitalism with left-wing emancipation creates a social monster that will destroy the people it encounters.

A frightened white middleclass man who reacts against foreigners is according to left-wing ideology an inferior person. It is however better seen as a sign that there is something wrong with society. Due to left-wing policies an important part of society and the public domain has become hostile to the white middleclass who are therefore excluded from opportunities that society could offer. The fear people feel when an environment is hostile to them is brushed aside by the left-wing elite. It is a clear example of blaming the victim. Instead of exclusion and by blaming the victim it is necessary to return them with their freedom and self-determination. This can be done by increasing the physical and psychological safety through coming down hard on crime and making sure society represents the white middle class again. As a result the mutual trust between people can be restored and an open society created for everyone. The hatred people feel against those who deliberately create a hostile environment in order to exclude potential competitors is comparable to the hatred the ANC leadership felt against the former Apartheid government in South Africa. Hatred is an emotion that is found in all people when they are deliberately wronged. It is therefore a 'good' emotion because it enables victims to stand up against their oppressor and fight for freedom.

The weakest in society are sacrificed to come to an ideal left-wing society. This utopia consists of a society whereby a small left-wing elite emancipates the rest. Emancipation is of course an euphemism for oppression whereby the left-wing elite can live a life of luxury which is based on the misery of others. This process should not be considered a simple conspiracy, in the sense of a one time deliberately coordinated action. It goes much deeper than that. It is the automatic result of a left-wing ideology that doesn't base itself on equality and self-determination but on a master-slave relationship. A left-wing calling; a colonial white man's burden as rationalisation for oppressing people so the elite can live a life of luxury. The left-wing religion can therefore be seen as a cynical, power-hungry and inconsistent ethical system, whereby others are sacrificed for a false ideology. The left-wing religion is therefore comparable to the 20th century competitors of Western democracy, like communism and National-Socialism.

3.1.2 Art and cultural imperialism

"I plead for an elite that explains what is good. Authority doesn't appear by itself, but I believe in the power of conviction. With enthusiasm and good ideas even the common man can be persuaded. You should not take the common man as he is now but what he could be."[x]

According to the elite the value of art lies in the fact that it offers people a perspective of a better world. How we can become a better person. Elitist art is therefore a form of emancipation, whereby the elite has to liberate the people from their ignorance. If emancipation was really the true objective of art then the common people should already be enlightened by now. The so-called emancipation through the arts is in reality a means of oppression whereby the people are made to believe that their world view is inferior and that only the elitist world view is worthwhile. Art is therefore used to impose a world view disadvantageous to the common man and at the same time offers the elite a platform to live a life of luxury at the expense of others.

A similar situation is also present in the world of literature. Literature consists of a confirmation of the world view of the elite and thereby has a high status. Only when a novel confirms the prejudices of the elite is it called literature. An often repeated theme in literature is the hypocrisy and narrow-mindedness of the ordinary people. Undoubtedly any country has some narrow-minded people but that doesn't mean it can be generalised to the entire population. It is a 'reality' that is preferred by the elite. There is in fact much more hypocrisy and narrow-mindedness among the elite then in the average population. The mere fact that literature is used to look down upon the ordinary person while it pretends to be enlightened is an excellent example. Much of literature is seen from the perspective of an outsider with which the elite can identify. According to literature this outsider is in reality superior to the rest of the population and demands its right to rise above the masses. It is thereby purposely ignored that it is the common man which is the real outsider and who has been marginalised by the elite. It's an ideal world view for an elite to legitimize its position. The majority of literature does therefore not reflect the nature of the people but of that of the elite.

Art is important for a society. Firstly, it is necessary to create a community and art gives it its identity, which is ever more important in a globalizing world. Secondly, art offers perspectives on how to live the best possible life. Good art also provides people with self-confidence. In order to win back the arts from the elite and its moral corruption it is necessary that subsidies are scaled back to a minimum. Those subsidies are in place because there is too little support for elitist art. True art can finance itself. By halting the flow of subsidies the art scene can be enriched and culture can represent the people instead of a small elite.

3.1.3 Multiculturalism according to Machiavelli

It is beneficial for an elite to have multiple distinct groups in society because it simplifies elite rule. The policy of divide and rule is easier when there is no single large group that can rise up to the elite. Furthermore, such a society legitimizes the existence of various distinct groups among which the elite-group itself. Something similar can be found in the political philosophy of Machiavelli who stated that one of the most important actions a ruler should implement to consolidate his power is to move foreign peoples to the area he controls. This drives a wedge and forms a barrier against potential resistance whereby the people are weakened. Imported foreigners will be friendly to, and allied with, the ruler because they need his support to make a living in a land where they don't yet have a network.

Resistance against mass-immigration is often labelled by the elite as racist and compared to the actions of the Nazi's during World War II. Furthermore, the left-wing elite also makes it illegal to try and work out a re-migration strategy in order to repair the damages. This is deemed ethnic cleansing and a crime against humanity. The left-wing elite has then created a system whereby friendly groups (the expatriates of the left-wing elite) are brought in by abusing the nation's legal systems and by expropriating the native population, materially, culturally and geographically. Any reaction against this policy is then outlawed. This is a clear example of selective justice and an important pillar of the imposed left-wing ideological prison.

3.1.4 Europe and the problem of identity

A serious threat to the continued existence of the self-determination of the people from European countries is the continuing expansion of the authority of the European Union. The supporters of the EU promote the rise of a European super state led from its capital, Brussels. This super state should then compete with other major world players like America and China. In order for this project to be a success the citizens of the European countries need to be endowed with a European identity. Europe is in the eyes of its supporters a project based on the values of democracy, freedom and human rights. It is interesting to note that this changes every few years. First 'Europe' was based on the desire to ban war forever. Then it was a project necessary to compete with the US, and so on. The mere fact that different arguments are used every time also is an indication that the arguments are false and hide the real objectives. According to the elitist perspective it is however of great importance that citizens consider the power of the EU as legitimate and thereby superior to those of individual member states. To this end the national identity of citizens has to be degraded and become subordinate to the European identity. No longer German or French, but European.

A problem in de-legitimizing national identities is that the project of Europe is based on the collection of historical and cultural identities of the various countries and regions. In order to make Europe a unitary or federal state these identities have to be eroded, but with it you erode Europe itself. This project will fail unless there is something especially valuable to replace the national identities. Another complicating factor is the presence of large numbers of non-European immigrants which dilutes both national and European identities and is replacing it with a new identity. It is highly questionable whether this will be a pro-European identity. Nationalism is in the eyes of Euro-fanatics the biggest enemy of the European project. Nonetheless there is much to say for the fact that it is these Euro-fanatics who try to pull away the pillars of European identity, namely its national identities, who are the biggest enemy of the European project.

3.1.5 Nationalism

Nationalism is an ideology that tries to bind the people to a political unit (the state) in such a way that the people, or the nation, coincides with the state; the nation-state. Those individuals who live in the area controlled by the state are nationalised to feel part of the people, which in turn is represented in the state. This is the elementary form of self-determination of a people. This description of nationalism is neutral but it often has a negative connotation which is mainly due to its association with World War II. However, ever modern state nationalizes its population because else it would not be able to gather enough support to implement effective policies. The population has to accept the authority and legitimacy of the state. This only happens when people believe that the state represents them. From this we can conclude that nationalism leaves no place for an elite to rule over the people. Nationalism is therefore one of the most important political movements to fight against oppression and to make sure that everyone has access to all positions within a society. Nationalism thus creates an open society for those excluded by the elite. Furthermore, nationalism is always based on a specific culture with which people identify.

The objective of nationalism is to have all members of the nation identify with the same culture. European countries do this by standardising the language, education, legal codes and media. In this way the less well off can no longer be excluded from important social positions. During the nationalisation process people are trained on how to correctly behave towards each other and the government. People need to identify with each other. A characteristic of nationalism is that it is a continuous process which is never finished.

Nationalism revolves around inclusion and not exclusion. The negative associations with nationalism are based on how it *could* be implemented, namely the exclusion and elimination of individuals and groups who are seen as outsiders. In light of the fact that the objective of nationalistic policies are to create one group, the exclusion of people is something not directly related to nationalism. In virtually all cases everyone within the influence of a state is nationalised. It is therefore more the rule that when some groups resist this nationalisation that resistance arises, like we see in independence movements.

Nationalism is a necessity for every modern state with its integrated institutions. It is furthermore crucial for individuals to experience individual freedom. If society disintegrates there is no longer an environment in which freedom can be experienced. It is therefore of great importance that the cultural community remains intact. Alienation from people's own culture reduces the individual freedom of citizens. It is therefore a necessity to reinforce the national culture.

3.2 Evolution as a description and explanation of life

One of the most important discoveries of the 19th century is the insight into the workings of evolution as formulated by Charles Darwin in 1859. According to Darwin's theory of evolution the diversity and complexity of life is the result of natural selection caused by natural circumstances in which the organisms who are best adapted to their environment survive while the rest dies out. An important element in this is the necessity for variation, whereby the organisms that have characteristics that give them a competitive advantage over others will survive and subsequently pass these characteristics on to the next generation. Since 1859 the theory of evolution has been expanded with new insights in genetics and molecular biology while the theory itself has stood the test of time. For example, Charles Darwin was unaware of the work of Gregor Mendel who was working on heredity. Darwin thought that characteristics of the parents were mixed in their offspring although genetics clearly shows this not to be the case. The idea that the survival of the individual is the most important factor in the theory of evolution has also been proven false. We now know that evolution is not about the survival of the individual or the group, but that the focus lies on the reproduction of genetic material; from *'survival of the fittest'* to *'inclusive fitness'*. The latter also explains the presence of altruistic behaviour which can't be explained with Darwin's theory of evolution. Helping others when there appears to be no self-interest is called altruism. When we look at evolution from the perspective of individual survival than altruism is always irrational because it only helps the other to survive at the expense of oneself. When we look at evolution on the level of the genetic material than it is actually rational to help others under certain conditions, even if this comes at the expense of personal survival. Children for example inherit fifty percent of their genetic material from each parent, while cousins and other relatives also share part of our genes. It will therefore be good for the survival of our genes to help those closest related to us.

The support can be increasingly greater with closer kinship. These improved insights into evolution can offer us a better picture of the influence that nature has on the social position and organization of man-kind in the world.

Social Darwinism has a negative connotation for many because it is associated with eugenics and was used to legitimize social inequality. These are some of the most important reasons why many reject the theory of evolution as a guiding principle in the design of a universal ethical code. Unfortunately people tend to forget that social Darwinism is only an interpretation of the theory of evolution and that politics doesn't get its values from evolution but that it uses Darwin's theory as a means to give other political ideals scientific credibility. Misuse like this doesn't mean that the theory of evolution can be ignored when trying to understand and explain social interaction. Firstly it is important to note that the theory of evolution is not an immoral theory but that it is an a-moral theory. The theory of evolution is a descriptive explanation of how the world works and is not a prescription of how the world should be organized. Although the theory of evolution doesn't know morality of itself it is still necessary that every moral theory is grounded in evolution or else we would get a theory that is detached from reality. Ignoring the principles of evolution would than be immoral because it would harm society which could have been prevented. Therefore evolution in a roundabout way is also a justification of the right life.

Much of the debate on integration and emancipation of minorities assumes an incorrect idea of the theory of evolution. Evolution works on the basis of the principle that organisms that are best adapted to current circumstances will survive. The underlying thought in much of the integration- and emancipation debate assumes that evolution is based on adaptation. This is similar to the theory of evolution that was dominant in the first half of the 19th century and had its main proponent in the person of Lamarck. According to Lamarck the long neck of the Giraffe was the result of stretching the neck by continuous generations of Giraffes. In human terms this can be compared with a man who is into bodybuilding after which his children will later also become muscular. This is of course incorrect and Charles Darwin showed that acquired characteristics are not inherited. Instead, evolution works on the basis of selecting those varieties that are most successful. When we look at the example of the Giraffe, we can see that there were Giraffes with long necks and with short necks. The long necked Giraffes had a greater chance of survival and had more offspring compared to the short necked Giraffes, which meant that the neck of Giraffes became longer over time. When we transpose this proven scientific theory to the ideology of equality as proposed by the Enlightenment than we see that the latter is incorrect. These ideals don't correspond to reality and the state of nature of humanity. In this way we create a society that conflicts with humanity and humaneness. The consequence of a society that is not made for people but for an abstract ideal is that persons who do not fit within this ideal are filtered out and will die out, as the theory of evolution of Darwin has adequately shown.

How should an ethical theory take the theory of evolution into account? How do we connect an a-moral theory with a moral theory? An ethical theory is a theory which proscribes the right way of life and indicates the morally correct way to deal with the world. According to most Enlightenment philosophers and their successors every ethical theory needs to be based on humanity and should provide for the best and most valuable life, in which 'best' and 'valuable' are defined in terms of success in the abstract philosophical system of Kant and utilitarianism. Because people, like all other biological organisms, function within the limits of the principles of evolution, it is necessary to ground an ethical theory in the theory of evolution. If we were to ignore this reality we would be building a theory without proper foundation, which unfortunately has happened many times. The theory of evolution can be compared with the theory of gravity. When an architect has a vision to build the greatest and grandest building of all time, he can not simply wish away gravity if the laws of gravity would hamper his design possibilities. Who would want to live and work in a building in which the designers did not take the effects of gravity into consideration? Such a building could be safe, but it could just as easily collapse under its own contradictions. The same applies to the design of an ethical theory. When we don't take evolution into consideration when designing an ethical theory than the ethical theory will eventually collapse under its own weight and cause many innocent victims. The denial that evolution stands at the basis of any ethical theory is therefore a denial of reality and is pure stupidity. Wishing away evolution is like wishing away gravity when you jump off a high building; you will not notice that your assumptions are wrong until you hit the ground after which it is too late. It is therefore not a question *if* an ethical theory should be grounded in the theory of evolution, but *how* this can best be done.

In what way can the theory of evolution show us what ethical system is fit or unfit if the theory itself has no morality and can therefore never be a justification for the choice of what is the right life? A description and explanation are not justifications and it is always an error of logic to reason from an *is* to an *ought*. Firstly, we can state that the theory of evolution disproves the theory of Divine inspired morality as well as Kantian ethics and utilitarianism, without the theory of evolution formulating its own ethics. The theory of evolution is therefore especially good at disproving social theories and is unable to establish its own normative system. The latter has been tried on many occasions and is known as social Darwinism. The problem with social

Darwinism is that many different and opposing values and arguments can be taken from the theory of evolution and that they eventually proved to be rationalizations of power hungry politicians. An ethics of evolution has therefore remained an illusion. Despite these failures it is nonetheless possible to ground human ethics in the theory of evolution if we assume that the facts and insights into the way the world works can help us to guide our moral instincts to better deal with the world. Although it is always an error in logic to reason from an *is* to an *ought*, it is also the case that an *ought* implies that it is possible. The comparison with the theory of gravity clearly shows this to be the case. The theory of gravity does not say what kind of building the architect has to design, but it does state the conditions that the design has to abide by. It is for example possible for a bird to partly defy gravity and to fly, but this is impossible for people. Millions of years of natural selection have led to a situation in which birds have adapted to flight. Wings, light bones, feathers and great physical fitness make it possible for birds to fly. People on the other hand do not posses these features and therefore make it impossible for them to fly without aid. The aids that people have developed in order to fly take these human limitations into account. It is therefore not people who fly, but it is aircrafts, helicopters or balloons that fly and create an environment that make it possible for people to fly along. Similarly, social theories should offer an environment that takes the limitations of people into account while at the same time enable them to overcome these limitations, like an aircraft enables people to fly without requiring any changes from people's innate abilities. Social theories should therefore take the limitations of human nature as developed through millennia of evolution into account. Hereby it is also good to realize that morality is not based on any physical law of nature but on an, although innate, social construction and therefore always relative without a direct connection to the factual world. If we therefore design a social system that goes against human nature than we have an immoral theory. When an ethical theory for example states that men and women are equal, and the biological structures would deny this, than we are stuck in a self-constructed social prison that will eventually destroy us because it damages our evolutionary fitness. The theory of evolution can therefore be seen as a *negative justification* that 'proscribes' what an ethical theory should not have instead of what it should have.

Why do we need a moral environment when nature itself is a-moral? We need morality because it enables us to know good from bad so we are able to see the threats to survival that are ever present. Nature might be a-moral, but we see everything that could be a threat to our continued existence as a form of evil. People create a social environment to mediate between nature and ourselves in which we need to survive. Without this social environment people are unable to survive. This also implies that a lack of social rules causes survival to be endangered. In that sense nature can be seen as evil, despite the fact that nature itself is a-moral. Nature is a threat to the survival of people if there is no mediating social environment, which makes nature part of evil, from the perspective of people. Fighting evil is therefore always necessary even though people's innate nature is good; i.e. positively inclined towards all those with whom we identify. In many respects nature has been pushed back with the advancement of human technological development when it comes to morality. When we look at the religions of hunter/gatherers we see that natural forces play a large role in their vision of good and evil. This is mainly due to the fact that the forces of nature play such a major role in the survival of hunter/gatherers. The more technologically advanced a society, the less influence natural forces have on the survival of people. In modern society natural forces are mostly replaced by a man-made and socially constructed environment as the greatest threat to survival. Perhaps technology itself will in the future become the greatest threat and most important source of evil.

The ultimate objective of biological organisms (within their limited existence) that live according to evolutionary principles is simply to survive in the sense of the guarantee of continued existence. An essential part of an ethical theory should therefore be survival. How this should be implemented in an ethical theory is not as straightforward as at first glance might appear. This is due to the complexity of life and the fact that the ultimate survival could even mean that a person looses his life. On top of this is the fact that evolution is short-sighted and that it does not have a long-term strategy. This means that those characteristics survive which guarantee the greatest success at the current moment, while characteristics that are less successful now but could provide a greater success in the future, don't survive. It should therefore be an objective of any ethical theory to enable people to rise above these limitations of evolution and become the ultimate survivor. We have the ability to look ahead and notice the pitfalls and adapt our social environment to a situation that lies ahead. This does not mean that we rise above evolution, but it does mean that we are better able to adapt to the whims of nature and increase our chances of survival. However, history has shown us time and again that the processes of evolution lead to ever more complicated and specialized life-forms, but that there are periodic fallbacks in which the most specialized organisms die out and the 'lower' organisms survive. The extinction of the dinosaurs is a good example of this, as is the extinction of the Mega-fauna of the last ice-age. Those animals that were best adapted to a certain environment and stood on top of the food pyramid died out. It is therefore incorrect to say that evolution means progress. The term progress is not applicable to evolution, because evolution has no purpose or objective. It is for example not an objective of humanity to rise above itself in order to become an Übermensch, just as it is not an objective of chimpanzees to rise above themselves and become human. This is rather an expression of self-hate in which we downgrade ourselves which can lead to self-destruction. An important difference between people and other animals is that people live in an environment that has been mostly created by themselves. This means that evolution doesn't stop, but that we can steer the way it applies to us to a certain extent by the choices we make on how to organize society. When doing this we need to prevent society becoming detached from reality, because that would make it difficult to react properly to threats from outside our self-constructed environment. There is inevitably a future, but it is not certain that humanity is part of that future.

3.3 Science and religion

3.3.1 Religion

For millennia religion has played a crucial part in organising society. Since the Enlightenment however, religion has officially been sidelined as being superstitious and irrelevant for organising a modern society. The (in)famous separation between church and state is one of the cornerstones of Western political organisation. Although this separation is seen as crucial to society, it is nonetheless misleading. It assumes the possibility of an amoral state which, as noted in previous chapters, is impossible because there always is a form of morality present in every human organisation. In order to see the role religion still plays we need first to define religion.

A widespread definition of religion is the following: "a set of beliefs concerning the cause, nature, and purpose of the universe, esp. when considered as the creation of a superhuman agency, involving devotional and ritual observances, and containing a moral code governing the conduct of human affairs."

Although this definition provides a good indication of what religion is, it also has its limits. For example, not all religions have a superhuman agency (like Buddhism). Furthermore, rituals and organisational structures are often completely different from one religion to another making it hard to determine when we encounter a religion. What is fundamental about religion is that God is the justification who needs no justification. His teachings are the principles upon which (the good) life should be based.

The problem that arises with trying to differentiate religion from other belief systems is that every system of belief and morality is ultimately based on assumptions which are considered self-evident; God is the justification who needs no justification, whereby the word 'God' can be interchanged with any 'self-evident Truth'. In the theories of the Enlightenment these Gods are self-evident truths like freedom and equality. These beliefs are taken to be Truths without the need to justify them; they are justifications of themselves. The moral value of equality or freedom is assumed to be good while no evidence is given for it. Of course if there were evidence for it, and therefore a justification, then it wouldn't be a principle, because it would be justified by something else. Ultimately, all belief systems are based on an assumption that is taken as self-evident, making all belief systems (non-)religious. There is therefore no real distinction between religious and non-religious belief systems.

Also the idea that Western society is based on scientific principles and therefore is based on facts instead of values is misleading and incorrect. Science only covers a small part of Western society, in the sense that although science is important for discovering nature's inner workings, the way that society itself is organised has nothing to do with science. For example, that most Western countries have elections every four years to vote for their political leadership is completely separate from any true scientific evidence. These ideas are often legitimated through pseudo-science, thereby using science's good reputation to convince people to accept these, inherently value laden, institutions. They are therefore not based on science but on the assumptions of the religious belief systems of the Enlightenment. Finally, science itself is also based on the assumption that cause-and-effect and time exist, making it ultimately a belief system as well.

Religion and Enlightenment

Islam is often labelled as outdated and incompatible with modern society. Especially the idea that Islam never experienced the Enlightenment is taken as evidence of its incompatibility with modernity. It is of course true that Islam never experienced *the* Enlightenment that profoundly changed Western culture since this was a Western phenomenon. This however does not exclude the possibility that Islam might have had its own enlightenment. The enlightenment of a culture can be seen as a process whereby its traditions and 'absolute' truths are critically re-evaluated and (religious) authority is questioned. When we interpret enlightenment in this way then the Western Enlightenment was not a one-off unique experience that only hit Western Europe in the 17th and 18th centuries. Through the ages many cultures have experienced enlightenment. The age of the great Greek philosophers, Socrates, Plato and Aristotle for example can also be seen as an enlightenment of Greek culture. The same can be said of many other cultures, including those influenced by Islam.

Another vision of the meaning of the term enlightenment is however less forgiving. The Enlightenment questioned the legitimacy of Christian doctrines and replaced them with its own, thereby degrading Christianity to the level of superstition. When we interpret enlightenment in such a way then it essentially means the replacement of one religious belief (Christianity) for another (the Enlightenment). Authority is then not only questioned but completely rejected in favour of a new one. In that case you are confronted with a completely new culture. If Islam would accept the Enlightenment as guiding principle of society then it would degrade itself to the level of superstition and Islamic culture would completely disappear in favour of the new Enlightened culture. This is essentially what already happened in Europe with Christianity when it was overtaken by the Enlightenment.

Many governments have placed restrictions on religious symbols in the public domain. These range from banning headscarves to removing Christian crosses from schools and thus preventing religion to be visible in society. The arguments for banning religious symbols are in part that the public domain should be culturally neutral in order for people with a different culture to not feel threatened. A religious symbol is then a provocation to everyone who has a different religion. As we noted in previous chapters, the public domain is never an amoral environment devoid of cultural values, because it is not based on the laws of nature but on those of man. The public domain is always filled with values. Outlawing religious values therefore means that they are replaced by other values. These 'other values' are always those that have the approval of the ruling elite and that favour their position in society. It is therefore their values that are labelled good and which are promoted in society.

Religion can be compared to language in that it disappears when it is expelled from the public domain. When all Christian symbols in the public domain are banned, Christianity will eventually follow. With it, an important pillar of peoples' identity will be blown away. Christianity will become a faith excluded from the public domain thereby giving it a lower status causing people to become ashamed of being Christian. When people are forced to hide their true identity, fear will rise sharply. In the chapter on fear it was explained that this can lead to depression. In such a situation fear can only be countered by anger and rage. Forcing people to hide themselves creates a large potential of aggression and violence. It is however not the intention of the elite to promote aggression and violence, but it is hoped that by banning Christianity from the public domain it will eventually simply disappear.

There is a great degree of agreement among socialists and liberals that religion needs to be completely removed from the public domain. In both these doctrines people are seen as atomised individuals without an identity, held together through a rational organisational body like a state. Despite the ideas of these *civil religions*, people are not atomised individuals and a person has to be seen as encompassing all with which he identifies, as demonstrated in the previous chapters of this book. When a Christian identity therefore is actively suppressed, all those who share this identity will be denied their existence, which causes great emotional stress. By denying people their identity they are by definition oppressed and limited in their freedom and life's chances.

Although socialists and liberals deny the relevance of identity and a value laden public domain, they nonetheless actively promote their own ideas and values, which can also be considered an identity. It is therefore safe to say that what they deny in others they demand for themselves. Banning Christian symbols from the public domain can therefore be seen as discriminatory. Discrimination always implies a hierarchical social environment in which the discriminated is seen as inferior. There are few avenues to combat this discrimination. Firstly, there is the possibility to give up the Christian identity and thereby recognizing its inferiority. A second possibility is to recognize the fact that you are in a zero-sum competition in which only survival is real and everything else an illusion. This way your identity is deemed valuable and victim of attack by an enemy that has dehumanized you. The objective is hereby to maintain the Christian identity and to make it a valuable identity which is in competition with other identities. This also means that mutual recognition and thereby the sense of community between groups has disappeared.

A third possibility is to try and convince others that it is unfair to deny Christianity its rightful place. The underlying feeling in such an action is always a form of indignation, which implies that there is a sense of community present whereby Christians are subordinate. Oppression will therefore continue as long as the Christian identity is not recognized as fully equal to others. This can only last as long as people have hope that they will eventually be recognized as equal. If this hope disappears, only the first two options remain; adopt a new identity or cancel the sense of community with the oppressor. When you wish to be democratic and equal to others then they can not have a different identity, because else they will be your master and you his slave.

Religion is always political

An often used argument to ban religion from the public domain is that it imposes a lifestyle upon people, thereby decreasing their freedom to choose their own lifestyle. Unfortunately, it is always failed to mention that other so-called civil-religions based on the Enlightenment are nonetheless imposed on society. Everyone who wants to participate in the *morally just environment* that demarcates society has to abide by a set of rules. These rules are based on the values of the various civil religions originating in the Enlightenment. They are therefore of the same nature as those of Christianity or Islam. In many respects, Western civil religions are identical to those of Christianity and

Islam. All of them are universal religions that try to dominate all aspects of society for all people. It is hereby different from ethnic religions like Judaism and Hinduism, which are exclusionary and only limit themselves to a specific ethnic group thereby denying their universality. In Western civil religions freedom, individualism and self-determination are deemed sacred and seen as good; while there can never be rational evidence for it. Just like God is sacred and the justification for all things in Islam and Christianity, so Western religions have their own Gods and practices.

Another argument used to ban religion from the public domain is the idea that it is impossible to formulate good arguments that can be understood by all if they originate in religious doctrines. The public domain is in this ideal an environment in which people can freely participate in a debate as equal participants whereby they can try to convince others of their position. This environment is assumed to be based on the values of the Enlightenment. As explained in previous chapters, this line of reasoning implies that everyone in the public domain accepts the values of the Enlightenment as legitimate. Arguments that use the authority of religion then do not necessarily have to be bad; they are simply not understood by people who do not share the same religion. This is an obvious example of false reasoning because banning a certain religion from the public domain is the reason why not all people understand (=accept as legitimate) arguments based on this religion. This argument would therefore simply vanish if religion would be brought back into the public domain. The reverse is of course also true. If a significant part of the people within a public domain were to reject the values of the Enlightenment as legitimate then arguments based on these values can no longer be used; the consensus over the fundamental values has then disappeared. It is therefore crucial for any religion to dominate the public domain if it wants to be accepted as legitimate.

Politics is about organising and legitimating a just society. Religion is therefore always political, because it does just that; proscribing how a just society should be organised. Differentiating between Islam and political Islam is then a misconception. If Islam were not political it could not be considered a religion and would simply be folklore put on display for tourists. Without a political component, Islam, and any other religion, is doomed to disappear. Eventually, a religion needs to try and become universal in order to survive. If a religion is not accepted as legitimate by the dominant group in the public domain then it can no longer be used as basis for arguments to organise society. The fate of religion is then similar to that of language in that if it is excluded from the public domain it will eventually disappear.

Survival is the justification that needs no justification

The world has many officially recognized religions. Furthermore, there are many more belief systems which are not labelled as being religious but, as we noted in the beginning of this chapter, should be evaluated in the same way as official religions. A crucial question is then what religion is best suited for society? As explained in the chapter: 'Evolution as a description and explanation of life', the ultimate objective of biological organisms is simply to survive. An essential part of an ethical theory should therefore be survival. A pre-condition for every religion is that the adherents of it survive; if there are no believers then there is no belief. In other words, not *God* but *Survival* is the justification that needs no justification and should therefore be at the heart of every successful religion.

A good religion therefore supports and promotes the survival of the people. A bad religion on the other hand harms the survival of its adherents and will eventually disappear. In this light, doomsday sects, but also much of today's Christianity in Europe and the (perverted) values of the Enlightenment, are hurting those who follow it, causing both the adherents and the religion as a whole to eventually disappear. Islam however promotes the survival of its followers, making it in that sense a good religion. Combined with the need for a moral belief system to base democratic institutions in, Islam can be seen as a strong competitor for the basis of modern society. One question then remains: How fundamental should a religion be? In other words, is there a need for a literal reading of Christianity or Islam or can it be interpreted? Fundamentalism argues that society should be organised according to the rules of that religion. Strictly speaking they are correct because if the teachings of the religion are not fundamental to society than they are not the true religion of that society but subordinate to another religion and are thereby mere superstition. As noted in the beginning of the chapter, what is fundamental about religion is that God is the justification who needs no justification and that his teachings are the principles upon which (the good) life should be based. A self-proclaimed Islamic state in which Islam is not the justification which needs no justification and where Islam is interpreted to fit society's political situation is therefore not an Islamic state.

3.3.2 Social science turned activism

In the 21st century, scientific evidence is seen as crucial in determining the legitimacy of a social system and an activity. This is mostly due to the fact that science has brought us all the technology and material comfort as well as the ability to be masters of the planet and to dictate nature instead of nature dictating people. Without science, our modern world would not be able to exist. However, social sciences should not be confused with real science. In genuine scientific evidence a physical law of nature is discovered and described which contains an absolute truth that is valid everywhere and every-time. Social science, like sociology, politics, economics etcetera, are in a completely different category because they don't describe actual physical laws of nature, but only the world as created by people; i.e. they describe the social interactions as they appear in society. These are dependent on values and as noted before, there is a distinction between fact and value. Even when social research correctly describes the innate human abilities they still can't be considered real science because a different environment will generate a different outcome.

In order to 'overcome' this innate contradiction in social science much emphasis is placed on the method of how the research is conducted. However, this emphasis on method is by definition misleading because it is impossible to completely rule out underlying values. For example, people don't start off *discovering something*, but always start from assumptions they have about what to look for and what needs to be achieved in order to solve a certain (perceived) problem. How such an assumption is constructed determines to a large extent the outcome of that investigation. Furthermore, many conclusions can't be justified by the research data, where correlations are often deliberately mistaken for cause-and-effect relationships.

Social science doesn't simply measure things but at the same time creates a new reality as well. By selectively doing certain research you are able to manipulate the outcome in such a way that it influences the opinion of the people in any desired direction. Social science can therefore easily turn into a means of oppression instead of a means to increase self-determination. This doesn't mean that social science isn't useful. On the contrary, social science is one of the West's most important achievements with which we can not only control nature but also ourselves. In order to have self-determination and thereby having our destiny in our hands we need to make sure that social science is free from abuse. Due to the fact that social science is always relative means that abuse is always around the corner. The scientific climate of the last decades clearly shows that a lot of so called science is based on left-wing activism.

There is no improvement in nature and all arguments that base themselves on improvement are therefore misleading. An 'advancing insight' is also an argument of power because it simply means that the opinion of the dominant group becomes more widely accepted as being the truth and not that we objectively come closer to the Truth. All social achievements, like equality of people and emancipation of groups are not based on true science but reflect the opinion of the dominant group in society. It also means that these 'achievements' are not set in stone and that they can be re-evaluated at any time.

Although social science is not genuine science it does rely on strong arguments to persuade people to accept the outcome as being a reasonable reflection of reality. However, when you sacrifice science you are by definition left with activism and activism has only one true argument and that is the argument of power. He who holds power holds the truth. Consequently, when an elite looses power it also looses the truth in favour of a new truth of a new elite.

'It is scientifically proven that intelligence is to a large extent inherited. It is also proven that oppressed people have a lower intelligence.' According to much 'social science' this clearly indicates that people who are oppressed are to blame for their oppression because they are simply stupid. It could of course also be the case that although intelligence is inherited it does require a productive and positive environment to develop and that oppression blocks this development. The elite of course favours the explanation that oppressed people are inherently stupid thereby legitimating their rule. This battle in the nature-nurture debate is a strong tool of deception by the elite and is used in virtually all social scientific evidence ranging from autism, to homosexuality to intelligence and self-confidence. It is not aimed at studying society but to create a justification for a desired left-wing society.

Much left-wing social science appears to be aimed at undermining self-determination in order to create a docile and fatalistic population. For example, nowadays every child who sometimes gets distracted is labelled as having ADHD which according to left-wing science can be traced to genetic factors. This means that free will is denied. Everyone who acts anti-social is also labelled with autism. The fact that the symptoms we label ADHD and autism also appear in every normal person when they are under stress and confronted with a hostile environment should give us an indication that the problems might not lie with the person himself but with society.

Suddenly science also proves that homosexuality is innate and not a lifestyle. This left-wing opinion is based on poor evidence gathered from unscientific studies and not by pinpointing specific genes that might be responsible. Left-wing evidence like the presence of lesbian sea gulls in Southern California should prove beyond doubt that homosexuality is innate. Unfortunately, studies like that are considered genuine and used to legitimate a social system. Gay rights activists should also be careful with support for left-wing evidence which proves that it is innate and a natural condition. Much of the, deliberately manipulated, left-wing studies do not show that it is a natural situation. Firstly, much of the data is accompanied by conclusions far distant from each other and sometimes even diametrically opposed. Left-wing scientific studies for example suggest that homosexuality is caused by chemicals and hormones in the early stages of development. These studies also note that it is a deviation from normal development.

Furthermore, there is a correlation between a subordinate social position and homosexuality. These conclusions are not welcome in a left-wing world view and are therefore redefined. This redefined world view is then imposed on everyone who wants to be part of the scientific establishment. Every scientist who does not subscribe to the left-wing ideology as being the absolute truth is endangering his career. The left-wing truth is more important than reality. Another example is that studies prove that most of the media is not left-wing. These studies are based on counting the number of left-wing and right-wing people and items. In the same way it is easy to prove that the Discovery Channel is in fact a propaganda machine for neo-Nazi's. When you count the number of times Hitler or the Third Reich is mentioned and compare that with the number of times American president Roosevelt is mentioned then the former exceeds the latter making the Discovery Channel, in left-wing social science style, a neo-Nazi propaganda machine. Pseudo-science is unfortunately deeply ingrained in all scientific institutions. Mass-immigration is also seen as a force of nature when it is obviously the result of policy decisions. The way in which we create and uphold laws determines to a great extent how many immigrants enter or leave the country and not some uncontrollable force of nature.

In conclusion, social science can be helpful in discovering possible insights into human nature and how best to survive. We should however always keep in mind that social science is in the end merely an opinion of people looking for a top-position in society and thereby ultimately relying on only the argument of power. Scientific evidence should therefore be seen as a tool that is used to determine which people hold legitimate power in society. It is then important to uncover if the research is focussed on your survival or if it is part of a zero-sum game whereby the other is bent on your destruction. As a defence against the arguments of the elite, that the scientific evidence can't be questioned, people should be aware that social science is merely an expression of literature carrying a high information density and nothing more.

Not self-determination but an inevitable destiny that we can't control is what people are told to believe. In this way the left-wing elite tries to create mindless slaves who bow down for a small elite. This is a radical shift with old left-wing principles where the ability to create a better society was at the core of left-wing ideology. If we would try hard enough, then we would be able to create a better world for all. It is clear evidence that the left-wing has become the establishment and has thereby thrown away all its principles. The interests of the establishment are always to create a docile and subordinate population. Power corrupts and power has completely corrupted the left-wing.

3.4 The freedom of association and the morality of exclusion

Is it allowed to give greater support to your family then to the rest of society? Can you place the interests of your children over those of others? In Western society virtually everyone agrees that responsibility for children falls firstly to the parents and not the community as a whole. The parents are liable when their children perform an illegal act. This difference between the family and the community implies the existence of a different morality between them. It is accepted as long as this difference doesn't limit the successes of others too much. If there were to be no difference at all than only the common culture would bind people together. The safety of family ties is then replaced by the competition of the individual. Furthermore, the state would become totalitarian whereby it enters every part of people's life.

Is a Jew racist because he is Jewish? Judaism is first and foremost a religion based on ethnicity and descent whereby everyone who is of different descent is excluded. Exclusion is in Judaism then discrimination on ethnic grounds. Despite this, Judaism is not illegal. Is it for people allowed to determine with what group they identify or should it be imposed by government? And what identity should people have? Is it racist to exclude others when they also have the ability to form their own group?

Every form of association necessarily involves excluding others who do not fit certain criteria. If a society accepts freedom of association it needs to accept that people form associations with people they identify and exclude those they don't.

People are social animals. An individual can therefore only be himself if he is part of a group. Individualism however is seen as an important achievement in Western culture and the idea that the group limits the freedoms and opportunities of the individual is widespread. In order to solve the contradiction between individual freedom and the necessity to have a community in which this freedom can be enjoyed, Western culture strongly emphasises the freedom of association. People are then able to decide for themselves to which group they wish to belong. If this freedom would be absent then a totalitarian state would be the only alternative and people would have to conform to an imposed culture. People are after all unable to survive as an atomised individual.

Freedom of association usually did not coincide with a specific identity previous to the large flows of immigrants to Europe. In the 21st century however many groups organise themselves on the basis of ethnicity. The multicultural society is an everyday reality. Left-wing activists consider it normative; the multicultural society is good. Everyone who is against the multicultural society is considered evil. Furthermore, it is (incorrectly) assumed that discrimination is a major threat to the multicultural society and that racism needs to be strongly condemned and outlawed. However, a multicultural environment is based on the existence of groups that organise themselves based on descent and affinity. A multicultural environment can't exist without discrimination based on ethnic criteria. The principle of discrimination can therefore never be bad in a multicultural environment because it is the foundation of that system, thereby labelling it as 'good'. In light of the fact that the term 'racism' is used as a moral judgment to state that the exclusion and prejudices of others based on ethnicity is evil, we can conclude that discrimination in a multicultural environment is not racism.

Indian culture differs from German or Italian culture. The world is multicultural. National states are to a large extent based on a shared culture of the people, thereby legitimating the structures of the state. If you would use left-wing reasoning then you would have to conclude that to follow the laws of any state would be racist. A state is in the end a cooperation between people who identify with each other based on an (imagined) affinity, thereby by definition excluding others somewhere in the world. A state by definition excludes people.

The national state nonetheless has proven itself to be a great vehicle to create freedom for everyone which is represented by it. The best example of this is the elite. The elite enjoys its privileged position and large freedom due to the opportunities the structures of the national state provide. In order to keep these privileges the elite distances itself from the common man who created the institutions and made the elite's opportunities possible. In this way the elite prevents the ordinary people from getting a good social position as well. The elite thereby undermines all of society's institutions that give the same elite their privileges. This is the ultimate example of the hedonistic, short term world view that is so characteristic of the elite.

In a multicultural environment it is necessary to strongly guard your identity in order to survive. The same principle applies on an international scale. The more international and open a society the stronger the identity needs to be to hold the group together. If the group disintegrates so do all the possibilities and freedoms.

4. TOLERANCE

Tolerance revolves around allowing different opinions and lifestyles to co-exist. In light of the fact that tolerance presupposes differences in lifestyle and opinion, we can conclude that a society in which we don't find these differences we also don't find tolerance.

An often heard remark is that the only thing that tolerance can't tolerate is intolerance. Tolerance is than perceived as a morally just environment. Only those opinions that respect the dignity of others (within this environment) deserve to exist within this environment. Violence is also unacceptable unless the environment itself is threatened after which violence can/should legitimately be used to defend this environment. Tolerance than is about leaving others their dignity, which is formalized in the Western notion of 'universal' human rights.

Even the most diverse and tolerant society still consists of one demarcated social system in which people compete for a limited number of high level positions. A successful career is also strongly correlated with happiness and evolutionary success. This means that people who are able to gain a high social position have a greater chance of seeing their genes survive. The ideology of tolerance states that people are free to determine their own lifestyle in order for them to be as successful as possible.

If for example someone 'invents' a certain lifestyle that enables him to become very successful in society this would make him evolutionary more successful than the rest. In order for the latter to survive they need to adopt this more successful lifestyle.

When the most successful lifestyle is adopted by all, the plurality in society dissolves and tolerance (temporarily) disappears.

Tolerance is however not an objective but a means to an end. The objective is to be able to continuously search for a better lifestyle/truth. Tolerance therefore revolves around a set of social experiments to find the best lifestyle. The experiment that provides the best results should then be adopted by the entire society. Due to the fact that we live in a dynamic world it is necessary to never stop experimenting. This means that there is always a need for some form of tolerance.

There is however also a completely different vision of tolerance which is mostly supported by the left-wing elite. Their argument is that it allows distinct population groups to co-exist without the need for them to identify with each other. In such a situation it is necessary that the public domain is devoid of specific cultural expressions that favour one of the population groups because it would limit the freedoms of the other group. Tolerance in a competitive society is only possible if the other person or group does not have a more successful strategy. It is impossible to be tolerant towards a superior group/lifestyle when you compete for the same means of existence because that would be suicide. In the case of group competition it is necessary to keep the group together and to form one coherent front against other competing groups. If that would not happen then the group would disintegrate and the individual members would loose the struggle for power. A major problem is that in order to keep a group intact its members need to abide by certain criteria. Those criteria define membership of the group. It means that these criteria are no longer available for members of other groups because they also need to be unique in order to demarcate their group boundaries. The situation then arises that a certain lifestyle has proven to be successful but people can't adopt it because it would threaten their identity and thereby endanger the continued existence of their group and thereby themselves. This means that in a left-wing multicultural society there are major obstacles to learn from others. Instead of providing elements for progress and freedom a multicultural society places restrictions on everyone.

In a truly tolerant society no-one should be able to monopolise a way of life because that would take away the only positive aspect of tolerance, namely experiment and adoption. A multicultural society is therefore never a tolerant society.

An important question is where tolerance ends. Does it stop with intolerance of others? In a competitive society the only true tolerance comes from the state. People compete with each other in order to obtain a good position whereby real tolerance is missing. If someone is truly tolerant towards a more successful person than he sacrifices his own success. People who claim to be tolerant often assume that their lifestyle is the best and that every other lifestyle in the end can't really be successful. Tolerance against those who are at the bottom of society is better seen as contempt or indifference.

Tolerance stops where the ability to be tolerant disappears. This means that if society threatens to disintegrate in competing groups tolerance should be replaced by intolerance. It is therefore a sign of tolerance to outlaw women's Islamic dress because it is a symbol with which people try to exclude all those who are non-Muslim and whereby identification with the rest of society is deliberately minimized.

5. THE RULE OF LAW

The law should be made by and for the people in order for it to be truly fair and just. Unfortunately, this has not been the case for decades. Although legislation is created by democratically elected politicians many of these laws were not designed with the best interests of the people in mind. Another issue is the implementation of regulations. A rule is never just a rule but always requires an interpretation. It can be interpreted in many different ways. A good example is the American Supreme Court. This Court is the highest court in the USA and consists of a group of judges appointed by politicians, who test the laws in order to see if they don't conflict with the constitution. The result of such a test is almost always dependent on the number of progressive or conservative judges in the Court. The results are therefore never unanimous and party affiliation is clearly visible. A similar situation exists in Europe with the major distinction that judges appoint themselves and that virtually all judges are left-wing liberals. The law is therefore consistently interpreted in a left-wing liberal manner despite the opinions of the people. This undermines the rule of law because the legal systems are in the hands of a small elite and not in that of the people. In order to regain democratic control of the judiciary it is therefore important that this monopoly is broken and power returned to the people.

Rules can always be interpreted in such a way that they are in someone's favour. The vaguer a law, the easier the interpretation and possible abuse. International treaties are virtually always vaguely worded in order to reflect the situation of an agreement between many countries that differ greatly from each other. In order to regulate the flow of migrants for example it is therefore not necessary to cancel international treaties. An important first step would be to change the way these laws are interpreted. Equality for example is always interpreted by the left-wing in such a way that positive discrimination is allowed while many laws strictly forbid it. In politics the phrase 'it is impossible' almost always means 'we don't want to do it because it is not in our (elitist) best interests'

5.1 The morality of the legal system

The law finds its origin in the morality of the community which makes it necessary for judges to take the morality of the community into consideration in their judgments. Judges therefore do not *implement* the law but *interpret* it in order to come to a fair and just judgment. The terms fair and just should therefore be seen as everything that does justice to the community whereby the cohesion and survival of the community is confirmed. The rights of the community are therefore ultimately more important than the rights of the individual victim or the perpetrator. In a democracy, judges interpret the laws that have been created by the democratically elected parliament. When the parliament is representative of the people, laws will be created that enable the community to prosper in freedom. In a true democracy there will therefore be an overwhelming influence of the people on the creation and upholding of laws for the community.

5.2 The separation of powers

Unfortunately, even the most democratic societies often have a large separation between the people and the judiciary as well as between the judiciary and the legislative. This situation is legitimized as being necessary to uphold the independence of judges and the law. It is an integral part in the separation of powers or the *trias politica* which is supposed to make a democracy a 'constitutional democracy'. A constitutional democracy should be able to offer protection against the dictatorship of the majority (=the dictatorship of democracy?). The idea behind the separation of powers is that the majority has to be protected from itself when they decide to create policy which is harmful to them, as well as to safeguard any minorities from the majority. It is in such a system the task of the elite, which appoints itself as independent arbiter, to impose justice upon the people. In light of the fact that justice is a reflection of the morality of the community means that the 'independence' of the judiciary (from the opinions and wishes of the people) means that it is not the morality of the people that governs, but the morality of the elite that controls the courts. What insights do judges have that the democratically elected representatives or the people themselves don't have? Judges base their verdicts on the laws, but it is the population that chooses the lawmakers to create laws that create the desired social order. When judges interpret the law in such a way that it does not reflect the wishes of the people then democracy is undermined and a democratic deficit is present.

The great advantage of having a separation between the judicial, executive and legislative powers is that it prevents abuse, not from the people but from the elite. Although politicians claim to represent the people, they often represent mainly themselves. It is therefore a threat to society that the (political) elite identifies only with each other and not with the people and tries to hold on to power in any way it can. This threat is ever present because the main objective of politicians is to gain power. By having a separation between creating the laws and executing them, a situation is created whereby the elite is unable to abuse its powers too much. The separation of powers is therefore mainly to make sure that one elite is unable to monopolize all power. Other elites have to be present to prevent one elite monopolizing power whereby these elites create a balance of power. This might be effective in preventing one elite to gain absolute power, but it also prevents the general population from controlling its own destiny and as such it is an enormous democratic deficit. A possible solution could be to have people elect judges as well as politicians. It is no threat to society when the judicial system is democratized. It is however a threat if undemocratic politicians try to influence justice for their own gains.

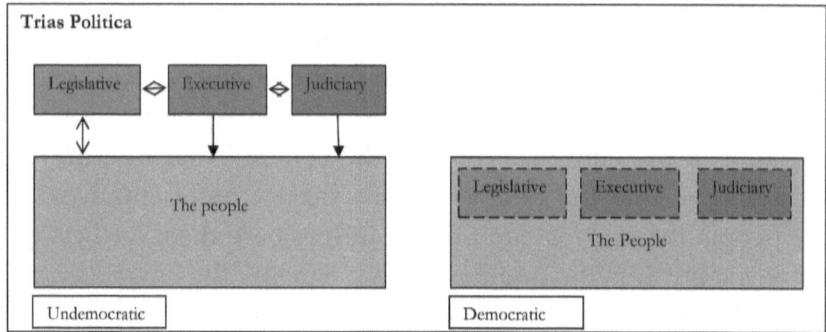

The judiciary is independent from the legislative but it is not impartial due to the fact that they form an elite by themselves and take the standards of this social group as basis of their morality.

5.3 Freedom under the law

In the final chapter we will see that the survival of the people stands at the foundation of democracy. This implies that the law is necessary to safeguard the survival of the people and to keep democracy functioning. It is hereby necessary that the laws are in the best interest of the population and not of those of the elite. This becomes clear when we look at the consequences of a law. A law creates a situation where potential possibilities in the community are transformed into real possibilities whereby the limits are demarcated. In this way it is possible to punish those who cross these limits and provide the rest the ability to profit from the offered freedoms. If laws favour the elite, or if they are interpreted in such a way as to favour the elite, than the elite gains freedom at the expense of the rest of the population, who are then less free. This limitation on freedom is due to the fact that a law also excludes other potential possibilities which can now not be realized. A law that favours the elite automatically harms the population and is therefore undemocratic.

5.4 Animal Rights

(Household) animals have fewer rights than people yet they are still safeguarded against abuse. We consider animals to (partly) belong to our community and award them rights accordingly. Besides rights animals also have duties. If a dog attacks an innocent person that dog can be lawfully punished (killed). In this way it is the duty of the dog not to attack innocent people. If he does attack than he looses his rights.

Furthermore, wild animals like whales are also protected from indiscriminate killing because we consider those animals to have the right to life. These rights have no duties attached, only recognition. We have expanded the community of those who deserve rights whereby we don't consider them to be fundamentally different. The differences between people and animals are not a difference in kind but a difference in the amount of characteristics they share. We have partly humanized animals and thereby enlarged our community.

6. FREEDOM OF EXPRESSION

The way in which we try to convince other people that our opinions on public policy are correct is in a democracy ideally done through debate in the public domain. In order to have such a debate it is necessary to have a certain degree of freedom of expression. A debate between people who share the same opinions is not a debate but a statement. We assume that a debate leads to one side being won over to the arguments of the other side. A problem is that a debate is by definition a competition and a conflict between people and/or groups. In a zero-sum competition it is imperative to hold on to one's own views and attack the other even if their ideas might be good as well. If we would not do this we would be overrun. Debate therefore enables people to speak but does not help them to be heard. In order to convince the other of the merits of your arguments there is a need for more than debate. Debate creates conflict and separation whereby consensus and mutual identification are needed to come to an adequate solution to the problems that a society faces.

Freedom of expression is necessary to enable people to voice their opinions. The more people are able to express themselves the better the chances are that the best choices are made available. The limits society places on freedom of expression are the result of what that society sees as the morally just environment and are thereby by definition relative. This relativity means that it is very hard to judge other time periods because of the different norms and values of the time. What a society regards as acceptable freedom of expression is everything which enables society to move forward in its quest for the best truth that guarantees survival. This means that it is by definition relative because nature has no concept of progress in the moral sense. Limiting freedom of expression is therefore due to perceived threats to (the elite of) society.

The idea that we reap what we sow is often used as an argument to keep unwanted opinions out of the public domain. It is true that opinions are able to spread because they are present in the public domain, but it is not the case that every opinion of every person will always dominate the public domain. On the contrary, most opinions are brushed aside as irrelevant or unwanted by the majority of the population. Opinions will quickly disappear if there is no fertile ground for them within the public domain. It is rare that an opinion creates its own fertile ground from scratch. There are for example always people who call for a revolution but this is almost always brushed aside as the ravings of the village idiot. In those cases that revolution really breaks out it is almost always the case that there was already massive support for the idea but that forces in society prevented these opinions from surfacing. The person who calls for a revolution is almost never solely responsible for an actual revolution but is primarily a medium that makes oppressed feelings and opinions visible and provides solutions for them.

A country or people which is under threat will often implement large limitations to their freedom of expression because they fear unity might disappear and with it society itself if conflict is allowed to roam free. This is a natural reaction but also makes it increasingly difficult to look for possibilities to escape from the oppressed situation. Strengthening of the public domain by increasing identification with each other is than the only option to keep the public domain free.

The outcome of a debate in the public domain clearly shows that this domain is full of values. A debate centres around the fact that other people can be convinced by arguments given by the opposite side. This can never be devoid of values because the objective is to convince others of a certain idea. Such a choice depends on the question if we value one argument over the other. As noted previously nature has no objective or values and only consists of facts and events. When we only take the facts into account there will not be a possibility to decide which facts are more important than others and why. This means that the democratic process as well as the outcome is filled with values. The power in a democracy has therefore strong links with the moral values that dominate in society.

Power is in a democracy usually more widespread than in a dictatorship. This doesn't mean that everyone has equal power. Nonetheless the power of the elite in a democracy is different than that of a dictator in a dictatorship. The power of the political elite is mostly given to them by the people they represent. This doesn't mean that the population has simply handed the power over to the elite. Representatives get their power by convincing the population that they are better able to deal with their interests. This is a continuous interaction between the arguments of the representatives and the interests of the population. Power is in an idealised democracy not clustered with the political elite but present everywhere. The fact that acquiring power is the main objective of politicians and that they have to do this in the public domain means that the debate in the public domain is not directed at objectively searching for the truth. Participants in the debate will try to win at any cost. Although power is distributed over large parts of society yet so is the abuse of power and the threats of violence.

A debate eventually leads to a truth that subsequently has to be implemented by government. Some see this truth as a consensus that was reached because everyone acknowledges that it is indeed the best choice. Unfortunately, this is only partly correct. Although it is the case that democratic government policy is supported by a large part of the population it is very rare that this support is universal. When the entire population would be in agreement of a certain decision than government would not have to implement policy to enforce it because everyone would do it anyway. This rarely happens. Despite this lack of consensus on the correctness of decisions there does exist consensus about the way in which the decisions have been made. There is therefore a consensus about the correctness of the process with which a decision is reached even if not all agree on the outcome of that process. We agree to disagree.

An often used argument to legitimate exclusion of people from the public domain is that "democracy is not for the fainthearted". People who are too afraid to actively participate in the public domain are then to blame for their own fear. In a true democracy there is no reason to be afraid because ideally all conflicts are meant to ultimately generate a social truth that benefits all. However, the fact that it is the victors in the public domain who determine the truth in a democracy means that people and groups who don't identify with the rest of the population have an interest in preventing others to actively participate. A very effective method to achieve this exclusion is to hijack the structures that make up the public domain and use these to instil fear in part of the population. Undermining people's identity, moral blackmail and power play, combined with actual physical violence is often very effective in excluding a large part of the population form the public debate. Clear examples of this are the threats, attacks and demonstrations by left-wing activists against all those who endanger the position of the elite. If you define fascism as political violence then Europe has been suffering from left-wing fascism for decades.

The law is based on violence to enforce regulations that not everyone agrees with (for himself). In order for the law to be considered legitimate the victims of violence need to agree with this violence. If this was not the case we would not have justice but instead have war. The fact that the public domain is completely filled with power and the ever present competition for more power means that dishonesty is more the rule than the exception. Democratic processes are often portrayed as fair and transparent, which they often are not. People with more power have the tendency and ability to manipulate the situation in order for them to get the benefits of the system. It is thereby important that the image of honesty remains intact in order not to loose the support of the population for the workings of the democratic process. If the support of the people for the democratic process disappears so does the consensus and the public domain itself. The feeling of justice is immensely strong and even takes precedence over our own best interests. Dishonesty like corruption should be dealt with in order for people to keep faith in the democratic institutions. If it continues to be unpunished democracy itself will eventually collapse.

7. DEMOCRACY

An important characteristic of a modern and free democratic state is that the public domain should be a-moral. In this way there is room for persons and groups who have differing opinions and ways of life to co-exist. The state should therefore not be ideological, because an ideology would infringe on the individual freedom of its citizens. We noted previously that nature is a-moral, while human co-existence is always normatively organised with distinctions between good and bad. Human co-existence is impossible in an a-moral environment. Furthermore, we noted that it is impossible to obtain values from facts. It is therefore surprising that the idea of an a-moral state is still seriously considered. The state is not a product of nature but is a social construction to help a community of people to live together. From here it follows automatically that the state always has a morality. If the state would not have a morality than people would not know what policy should be implemented because there would be no sense of what is important and what is not. It would therefore be detached from social reality.

The fact that the state always has a morality has major consequences for the way in which we have to look at the public domain. The public domain has a moral basis. It is therefore not the case that the public domain acts like a vacuum or buffer zone which gives people the freedom to have their own beliefs without limiting the others in their beliefs. A public domain which is vacuum of values creates a complete isolation of the individual from every other individual. Taking into account human nature with the Self as elementary building block, this would mean not only an alienation from the other but also an alienation from oneself. If people see 'rationality' as something a-moral and rational-scientific than this rationality does not mean greater freedom but in fact acts like the opposite because people are isolated from a valuable existence in a moral environment.

7.1 Democracy as a procedure to discover a Truth

The reasons for why some people plead for an a-moral democratic state is partly due to the way democracy is defined. In everyday speech democracy is seen as the rule of the people over themselves. Democracy is than opposed to other ways of government whereby only one or a small group rules. The democratic state is thus based on the desires and interests of the people. In political science, democracy is somewhat differently defined than simply the rule of the people, by the people and for the people. According to the most common political theory the essence of democracy is not a specific defined content but it is the procedure to come to a result, a Truth, whereby the democracy in itself has no objective other than the creation of the public domain in order to make the search for Truth possible. This public domain than has to create an environment in which all persons have the ability to participate in the public debate as equals in order to get to the best possible truth together. To this end the public domain should not be based on a morality and should also be devoid of power. The conclusion that follows from this theory is that democratic procedures should be a-moral and without objective. When people decide to justify and legitimate the democratic procedures by formulating an objective for them, then democracy itself is denied and should therefore be seen as an undemocratic act. It is than not the people that rule but it is a certain Truth that rules. A democracy can therefore not be based on a Truth but should instead be undetermined and empty of values. In a democratic society people will be continuously searching for new truths that are constantly being formed in the public domain ensuring that there will never be one Truth that comes to sit at the basis of democracy. In this line of thought it is assumed that any truth can be lost but that being directed at getting to the truth will always remain. This is therefore a Truth of democracy. It subsequently provides the ultimate negation of left-wing claims that their ideology should be the basis of modern Western society. If left-wing ideology governs then democracy is denied.

7.2 Survival of the People as Truth in a democracy

Nature is based on physical laws of nature, but the human world is always based on values. In light of the fact that democracy is not a physical law of nature but that it is a social form of organisation by people means that democracy can never be devoid of values without it becoming worthless. The idea of freedom for example is essential for the democratic process to function properly and is strongly connected to values and ethics. Freedom is not an object that we own but is a possibility to do something. In order to have freedom we need to have an idea of what the right choice is, meaning that we need to have a sense of good and bad. If we did not know right from wrong than we would not know what to do and our freedom would be an illusion. In order to have freedom you need to have a morality. This implies that there should be a morality within the democratic procedures because else freedom can not exist and therefore democratic debate would not exist either.

Morality is the result of evolutionary selection to maximize survival. The foundation that lies underneath the freedom to do something as well as underneath the democratic procedures that make the search of society for truth possible is than to maximize the survival of the individual and the community. Democracy therefore should be based on an underlying truth and the procedures and process should have a morality. This morality should however not be a left-wing ideology which glorifies the elite, but be based on a national identity which guarantees successful survival for the people.

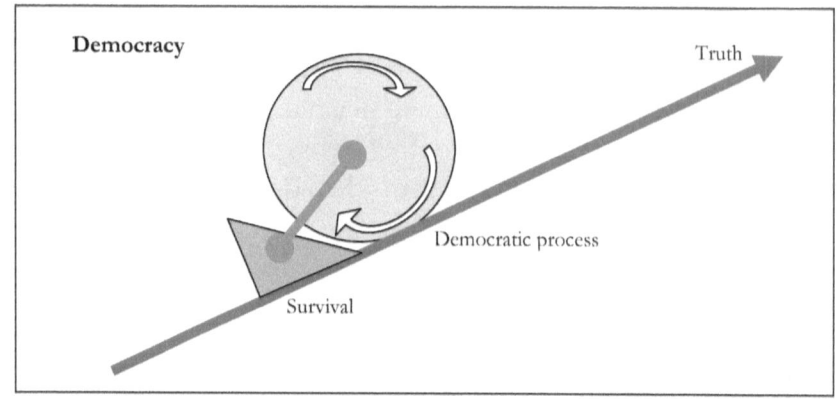

A second reason why people plead for an a-moral and neutral state is because it is deemed necessary for the co-existence of different ways of life within one political unit without there being an imposition of an ideology upon individuals. This line of thought assumes that people are completely autonomous individuals. Others are than not necessary and are even a limitation to the freedoms of the individual. However, people can never be themselves without interaction with and recognition of others. In order to have freedom their needs to be a well functioning community in which this freedom can be enjoyed. Individualism is therefore not the objective but only a means to get a good social position within a community of significant others. The public domain is always full of values that influences everyone in it and defines the identity of the people to a large extent as well. The fact that many deny the morality of the public domain does not mean that the morality somehow doesn't exist. It is more an indication of the great success of the indoctrination of the people. As long as all people within the state's borders share the same national identity there is one people where individuals have great individual freedoms and live under a law they created and is in their best interests. If certain identities become more influential than the national identity then democracy itself is critically undermined and will eventually disappear. In order to save both democracy and the constitutional state it is necessary to impose a primary identity on everyone.

7.3 Political parties and the demarcation of the public domain

Many claim that the democratic process should be devoid of values and morality in order to be truly democratic. Political parties on the other hand are based on an ideology from which they perceive society. Proponents who claim that democracy should be without morality and that political parties are necessary for democracy to function usually pretend that parties are simply participants in the debate, like every other person or group. In that way it is claimed that democracy itself is without ideology while there is the possibility to freely choose one or more of the ideologies that political parties represent. Unfortunately this reasoning is incorrect because the environment in which political parties have to operate is demarcated by the 'morally just environment'. It is for example not allowed for a political party to have 'anti-democratic' principles. Those parties are excluded from the public domain and debate and are usually outlawed. The idea that the debate is completely free and open to all people and opinions is therefore incorrect. The conditions to participate in the debate are determined by the degree to which these ideas are within the limits of the morally just environment. In light of the fact that these limits are determined by the dominant powers in the public domain means that the debate is tilted in their favour. Ideas which might provide a better solution for problems in society but that are damaging to the elite therefore rarely enter the public domain or only with great difficulty. The problems however do not disappear and only increase their potential harm to all those who are not part of the elite.

Western democracy is based on the values of the Enlightenment which means that only ideas and activities approved by it are allowed to enter the public domain. It is therefore the

Enlightenment that governs and not the people. The values of the Enlightenment, like all values, are not absolute but are nonetheless implemented as though they were absolute. Much policy is implemented that although good from the perspective of the values of the Enlightenment is not always good for the best survival of a large part of the population. Where people warn against a possible take-over of democracy by a Truth that could eventually lead to a dictatorship we are faced with the reality that this already is the case for all of Western democracy. The correct warning that a wrong truth can lead to the demise of the people is ignored and surrounded by a taboo.

Political parties are not simply powerful players in the public domain but are actually responsible for the creation of much of this domain. It is for example the debate within political parties that determines a large part of the Truth. This debate is the exclusive domain of politicians from the particular parties. The debate in the public domain is therefore to a large extent a debate between politicians of the various parties who then come to form a Truth without a major role of the majority of the population. Political parties themselves are a public domain for the politicians of the particular party. An individual politician has to look for solutions for society's problems from the preconditions of the ideology of the political party. If a politician no longer reasons from the ideology of the party then he is left with the option to step out of the party and create his own party or by defecting to an established party with a different ideology.

Deviating opinions are mostly excluded from the public domain before their validity can be tested. In this way renewal is crushed before it even surfaces. A large degree of consensus is present that the current truth is the only correct truth and that there is no need for 'revolutionary' ideas. The problem with this is that there often is no need for new ideas before these ideas exists. For example there was no need for Internet before it existed while no-one can live without it today. This also applies to political ideas. The ruling political elite has vested interest in preventing the rise of new political ideologies and parties because it would undermine their position. The political establishment therefore supports the status quo where it comes to political ideologies. Besides the support of the establishment it is also the Enlightenment principles that lie at the foundation of our democracy which are responsible for the fact that the old ideas still dominate the debate in the public domain. These theories, from socialism to liberalism, are best suited for an environment in which the Enlightenment principles are absolute because their values are derivatives of it.

Modern political parties generally have two distinct functions. The first function is to mobilise the people and to convince them that the ideology the party promotes is correct. The multitude of parties uncovers differences present in the population and partially creates these oppositions as well. The political party that is able to convince the population the most will receive the majority of votes. This is the appearance of the political party as a missionary organisation. The second function of a political party is to govern. The appearance of the political party as bureaucratic organisation. This function is in many respects the opposite of the first function because instead of emphasising differences the political party has to govern on the basis of rules that are applicable to all. In everyday practice this usually means that when a political party has received its votes on the ticket of a specific promise and ideology it will throw these principles out the window and will focus on power politics. Political parties are therefore more often a way to recruit and educate future political leaders than that they are representative for the population. Bureaucratisation of politics is therefore also a sign that the political establishment has no need to convince the people of the legitimacy of their dominance because it is taken for granted.

One of the main tasks of political parties is to uncover and create differences in order to have a truly democratic debate whereby it is possible to discover new truths. It is therefore senseless to claim that a political party should not be allowed to exclude groups, lifestyles or ideas. Prioritizing one thing over the other in order to create the best possible society is one of the pillars of the democratic system.

In the battle for political power it must be assumed that politicians don't primarily operate from the perspective of the people's best interest, but from their own best interest. In case politicians don't identify with the population than democracy disappears.

The public debate is thus primarily controlled by politicians who strive for power and a good career and who have to do this in political parties with distinct ideologies. This in itself is already a limitation of the democratic level of modern democracies. The true democratic deficit however goes beyond that. An environment with power hungry politicians basing their actions and visions on party ideologies is not necessarily undemocratic. Citizens still have the choice what political party they wish to support and anyone is able to establish his own party. Unfortunately, this is mostly theoretical. Virtually all political parties have a long history and new parties usually quickly disappear. Most political parties have ideologies like socialism, liberalism and conservatism that are mainly rooted in the 19th century. The fact that these parties are so long-lived can indicate that the ideas upon which they are founded are good. It could also be that political parties use their power to exclude others and organise the public domain in such a way as to favour the establishment. Furthermore, the will of the people is often manipulated and finally it is also the case that the public domain essentially is an Enlightenment environment that favours the established parties.

To some it appears as if political parties have no ideology and only operate on the basis of *realpolitk*. An example to back this idea is the big difference between present-day socialism and the same ideology thirty years ago. There is undoubtedly a major difference between socialism, liberalism and conservatism now and in the past but this doesn't mean that the ideology has disappeared. The ideologies have not disappeared but they changed to better fit current day society. This indicates that the general public has an impact on the interpretation of the ideologies. It also indicates that the public domain is for a significant part to be found within political parties because much of the change has occurred through internal debate on how to renew the party. Political parties have the monopoly on the most important government positions which provides them with great power to manipulate the public opinion. Combined with the fact that the political debate in the public domain is primarily waged by politicians as well as the tendency of people to vote for people they know means that it is very difficult for new parties to arise and become part of the political landscape.

The way in which the political leadership in a democracy is checked is through voting them out of office when they have implemented bad policy. It might appear reasonable to vote the political leadership out of office in order for the people to have control over the policy that they want to have implemented. Although it is correct that this threat means that the political elite has to take the opinions of the population in mind it is unfortunately not the case that the people control the politicians. As we noted previously the objective of the democratic process is that through a debate people come to a Truth and that this truth consequently is implemented by appointed/elected officials. The people's representatives in a democracy have a certain power but this power is dependent on what they say and do. An important question in this is what representation means.

There are two different definitions of representation when it comes to democracy. The first form of representation is delegation whereby the representative reflects and literally executes the wishes of the to-be-represented group. The second form of representation is different. It is possible for a representative to be a reflection of the group he represents without him being a mere messenger of the group. It is similar to a painting of a landscape which is a reflection of that landscape without it being a copy of it. Instead it enables a truth to be seen that is objectively not present. It creates a truth. This is also how much of the representation works in politics. The truth which is present in politics is partly created by the politicians themselves. Political parties and politicians try to gain power in the public domain. To this end they try to uncover feelings present in the population and subsequently name and manipulate them. The reason why people are searching for a truth is that it hasn't been found yet. There is therefore a sense of vagueness and indeterminateness in the public domain. This vagueness causes insecurity and fear among the population. The best way to handle this fear and insecurity is by labelling the danger, because it is difficult fighting shadows. It is unfair to brush away the fear for societal shadows as irrational, because shadows can be dangerous. We just don't know which ones are dangerous and which are harmless. Uncovering and labelling problems is therefore a crucial part of the task of a politician, because vague and indeterminate feelings present in the population become a reality through this labelling. The fact that politics plays a big role in creating the truth causes a system whereby the population judges its politicians afterwards to be by definition unreliable. How can it be possible to judge a politician whether his actions were good in the sense that they were in accordance with the truth as the best interests of the population, when it is in large part the politician himself who is responsible for creating this truth? Herein lies an ideal element for abuse and misuse by politicians that is eagerly used by them. As we noted previously the most important motivation of politicians is to gain power. It is therefore relatively easy to legitimate political manipulation because it is an integral part of a system that is seen by most to be legitimate and perhaps not perfect but the least bad one of all.

7.4 Populism

Populism assumes a direct connection between politics and the people. In populism there is no mediation of civil society and it is also not necessary that there is a public discussion about certain subjects whereby personal issues, problems and ideas transform into a communal truth. Furthermore, populism approaches politics from the perspective of the people and not from that of the elite. It also recognizes that the will of the people is denied by the (political) elite.

Populist politics understands that the existing procedures that ought to guarantee democratic debate and transfer of power have been hijacked by an elite, causing democracy to disappear. The search for the best truth for the people can therefore only take place outside these hijacked institutions. Populism is about regaining democracy by circumnavigating the hijacked, and consequently dictatorial, institutions and replacing this with a direct connection with the people.

Established political parties assume that the best form of politics is when a political elite proposes its political values and solutions for society after which the population is given the opportunity to vote for one of them. Populism turns this procedure around whereby the population has certain values and possible solutions which they want politicians to address and solve. The fact that populism takes the problems of the population as starting point makes it potentially a very democratic political model. There are unfortunately several disadvantages of pure populism.

In previous pages we noted that in a democracy the truth is sought through discussion in the public domain. An important task of politicians herein is to formulate ideas and arguments that address the problems living in society and thereby making these problems visible after which they can be dealt with. Such a quest for a Truth is not present in pure populist politics whereby the debate is skipped and the population is directly represented, which lead some to question the democratic nature of populism.

Opinion polls are also populist methods because they imply a direct connection between the individual citizen and politics. Some established politicians therefore claim that even opinion polls are a danger to democracy because they don't go through the proper procedures. Others see opinion polls as an important asset to democracy because it allows politicians and the population itself to get a better insight in what the views of the population really are. This allows the political elite to adapt its policy accordingly. American politics is a good example of this.

There are however also negative aspects of populism. Populism can for instance easily lead to corruption whereby an influential person has direct contact with the populist politician in order to have him solve a particular problem he has. A populist politician is of course unable to implement the desires of everyone he encounters because there are as many different problems as there are people. A pure populist approach could therefore quickly lead to corruption and power-politics, especially because a populist politician is not bound by a particular ideology. The policy of a populist politician can quickly lead to power-politics whereby he is not driven to address the problems of the population but driven by the desire to hold on to power. Populism will then be destroyed by its own contradictions.

Even if the populist politician can resist the temptations of power-politics the problem remains that the population might not know what is good for them. It is paternalistic and often misleading to claim that the elite knows what is best for the people while they themselves do not. The way our society is organized nonetheless makes it partly true. Through the manipulation of people's will, it often happens that people don't know what they really desire or that people desire things that go against their own interests. When a populist politician only executes the will of the people the resulting policy could be against the best interest of the population even though they desire the specific policy and are incorrectly assuming that this policy is the best one.

It is therefore essential that populist politicians not simply act as the spokesperson of the people but that they also make the invisible problems that haunt society and hamper the ability of the people to make informed decisions on what is their best interest visible. By addressing these invisible problems the populist politician at the same time creates the truth and not simply acts as a spokesperson. A genuine populist politician therefore has to address the problem of the oppression of the will of the people and make it visible in order for the population to make the best informed decision. This leads us to the previously discussed issue of the vagueness and indeterminateness of society and the potential dangers of societal shadows.

Many social problems are like shadows that undermine a successful life for the people. As long as these problems are not labelled there is no possibility to address them and so they remain like shadows continuing their destructive work in the background. These shadows are not harmless or irrational because they create a fear that is completely justified because every shadow can be lethal but you never know which one.

The argument that it is the politician who creates the truth is only partly true because it is not the case that when a politician doesn't label the problems they consequently don't exist. The problems remain but in their shadowy form and are an even bigger threat then if they would be labelled. If problems are not labelled they remain active but possible solutions to these problems don't have the ability to arise. Those possible solutions could very well be to address the oppression by the elite. The solution to the problems of the population could then become a problem for the elite which of course has enormous interests in making sure that the problems of the population never transcend their shadowy existence.

The populist quest for truth is then to reason from the perspective of the people and have their best interests in mind and to create policy based on this. An important part of this populist quest for truth is to uncover hidden problems that hinder the people in making informed judgments about the situation. In such a scenario the populist politician speaks the language of the people and at the same time adds to its vocabulary unlike the elite which speaks a different language.

The main difference between populists and other politicians is that the former reason from the perspective of the interests of the people while others take the perspective of the elite by looking out for their best interest only or what the elite thinks is best for the people. The populist politician can therefore be seen as a champion for the emancipation of the unrepresented whereby the 'silent majority' are given arguments to overcome the intimidation by the elite. The silent majority is most often silent not because they agree with everything but because they lack access to the proper arguments which is caused by their exclusion from large parts of the public domain.

NOTES

This book is a translation of **"Het Verlichtingskabinet"** with ISBN 9789080876897

ⁱ "Allen die zich in Nederland bevinden, worden in gelijke gevallen gelijk behandeld. Discriminatie wegens godsdienst, levensovertuiging, politieke gezindheid, ras, geslacht of op welke grond dan ook, is niet toegestaan."

ⁱⁱ "Het in deze wet neergelegde verbod van onderscheid geldt niet, indien het onderscheid een specifieke maatregel betreft die tot doel heeft vrouwen of personen behorende tot een bepaalde etnische of culturele minderheidsgroep een bevoorrechte positie toe te kennen ten einde feitelijke nadelen verband houdende met de gronden ras of geslacht op te heffen of te verminderen en het onderscheid in een redelijke verhouding staat tot dat doel."

ⁱⁱⁱ 'Mijn probleem met Wilders, en dat is zó cruciaal dat ik niet met hem wil samenwerken, is dat hij onderscheid maakt op groepsgronden, tussen mensen die daar helemaal niets aan kunnen doen. Hij raakt de kern van onze rechtsstaat.' Job Cohen in debat met Rutte, 28 mei 2010 (http://www.volkskrant.nl/vk/nl/2686/Binnenland/archief/article/detail/1000727/2010/05/28/De-markt-heeft-geen-moraal.dhtml)

^{iv} "Een vrouw vergadert over het algemeen efficiënter en heeft minder behoefte om eerst haar eigen ego uitgebreid [te uiten] dus uiteindelijk ben ik ervan overtuigd dat een vergadering korter duurt dan wanneer er geen vrouwen bij zijn. Het duurt korter en gaat meer over de inhoud." Neelie Kroes in een interview met Jeroen Smit voor het programma Leiders gezocht (http://educatie.ntr.nl/leidersgezocht/)

^v "De diversiteit in de samenleving is niet de gestuurde of beoogde uitkomst van vakbekwaam beleid. Het is een gegeven van de moderne samenleving, waarin wij ver reizen en steeds weer elders gaan wonen; en niet alleen wij. Die diversiteit geeft, net als wijn, smaak aan de samenleving. Als ik slechts klonen van mijzelf op straat tegenkom, is het niet de moeite waard om naar buiten te gaan." Toespraak van de

Minister van Binnenlandse Zaken, Piet Hein Donner, tijdens de Denk Divers dag op 18 november 2010

(http://www.rijksoverheid.nl/documenten-en-publicaties/toespraken/2010/11/18/minister-donner-geeft-in-toespraak-visie-op-diversiteitsbeleid.html)

[vi] "Het is een simpele *business case*. Om onze klanten goed van dienst te zijn, moeten we ook een afspiegeling van ze zijn" Alexandra Philippi – Directeur HR bij ABN Amro

(http://www.mt.nl/157/25841/magazine/manager-abn-meest-vrouwvriendelijk.html)

[vii] "Diversiteit wil zeggen dat we als organisatie een dwarsdoorsnede van de maatschappij zijn." Jitka Beukenkamp – Cap Gemini (Management Team 20, 17 december 2010; People matter, results count p45)

[viii] "Waar vrouwen in de praktijk vooral tegen aanlopen zijn de oude structuren en het langlopende netwerk van old boys dat ook binnen een grote organisatie ontstaat." Henk Noort, columnist voor Het Financieele Dagblad.

(http://www.mt.nl/157/25841/magazine/manager-abn-meest-vrouwvriendelijk.html)

[ix] "Vrouwen die een hogere opleiding afgerond hebben, zijn er vaak van overtuigd dat ze de wereld kunnen veroveren. Als ze dan in een organisatie komen waarin de cultuur toch net iets anders is dan ze verwacht hadden, tast dit hun zelfvertrouwen aan." Nina Skorupska, Raad van Bestuur van Essent. (Management Team 20, 17 december 2010; Energie steken in de carrièrekans van vrouwen p48)

[x] "Ik pleit ook voor een elite die zegt waar het op staat en die helder uitlegt wat kwaliteit is. Autoriteit komt niet vanzelf, maar ik geloof in de kracht van de overtuiging. Met enthousiasme en goede ideeën zou zelfs die 'gewone man' zijn over te halen. Je moet niet uitgaan van de gewone man zoals hij is maar van hoe hij zou kunnen zijn." Anna Tilroe in NRC Handelsblad van zaterdag 11 september 2010 over kunstsubsidies

www.ingramcontent.com/pod-product-compliance
Lightning Source LLC
Chambersburg PA
CBHW031301280526
45784CB00004B/1937